D0025734

Television
Production
Workbook

◼ FROM THE WADSWORTH SERIES IN BROADCAST AND PRODUCTION

Television
Production
Workbook

ELEVENTH EDITION

Herbert Zettl

San Francisco State University

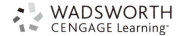

Australia • Brazil • Japan • Korea • Mexico • Singapore • Spain • United Kingdom • United States

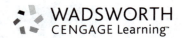

© 2012 Wadsworth, Cengage Learning

ALL RIGHTS RESERVED. No part of this work covered by the copyright herein may be reproduced, transmitted, stored, or used in any form or by any means graphic, electronic, or mechanical, including but not limited to photocopying, recording, scanning, digitizing, taping, Web distribution, information networks, or information storage and retrieval systems, except as permitted under Section 107 or 108 of the 1976 United States Copyright Act, without the prior written permission of the publisher.

For product information and technology assistance, contact us at **Cengage Learning Customer & Sales Support, 1-800-354-9706**. For permission to use material from this text or product, submit all requests online at **www.cengage.com/permissions**. Further permissions questions can be emailed to **permissionrequest@cengage.com**.

ISBN-13: 978-1-111-34791-8
ISBN-10: 1-111-34791-3

Wadsworth
20 Channel Center Street
Boston, MA 02210
USA

Cengage Learning products are represented in Canada by Nelson Education, Ltd.

For your course and learning solutions, visit **www.cengage.com**.

Purchase any of our products at your local college store or at our preferred online store **www.cengagebrain.com**.

Cover Image: © iStockphoto.com/craftvision

Printed in Canada

1 2 3 4 5 6 7 13 12 11 10

To all the students using this workbook,
which is meant not to reprimand you for what you don't know
but to help you identify what you need to learn

Contents

CHAPTER 3 The Script W-35

CHAPTER 4 The Director in Preproduction W-45

Preface

This preface is divided into two parts—one for the student and another for the instructor—to facilitate giving each party specific and relevant information.

▨ FOR THE STUDENT

The *Television Production Workbook* is designed to help you learn the rather complicated subject of television production. To move from being a gifted amateur to a true professional who understands the finer points of video and is able to produce high-quality work consistently, you must go beyond talent and innate skills. The *Workbook* will help you accomplish this task in two ways: by reinforcing the information that you have read in the *Television Production Handbook* and by revealing what you still need to learn.

If you could correctly fill in all the bubbles in the *Workbook* without using any outside aids, you would be eligible for an advanced class. Assuming that you are not quite there yet, this workbook is laid out for ease of use and optimal learning. Here are some of its main features:

- ▪ Each chapter begins with a review of key terms that tests your understanding of the chapter's basic terminology.

- ▪ The middle section of each chapter offers a variety of objective questions and production diagrams to analyze. The aim is to help you recognize and apply the production principles discussed in the *Handbook*.

- ▪ A true/false review quiz tests whether you can recall the basic terminology and specific production principles.

- ▪ The problem-solving applications at the end of each chapter are intended to enable you to apply the material you have learned to typical production situations. Your instructor will probably come up with many more examples—all in the interest of making the translation from classroom learning to field application maximally efficient and effective.

You will discover that the problems in each chapter differ considerably in degree of difficulty. Some are designed simply for quick recall, others for a more careful weighing of several possible options. Don't get overconfident when you can correctly answer the more obvious questions; you may miss the answers to the more demanding ones. Be aware that some of the problems require the filling in of two or more bubbles. In such a case, the problems that need multiple bubbles are clearly indicated.

Dealing with a workbook is similar to being involved in extensive preproduction activities: both at first seem somewhat irrelevant or at best time-consuming busywork.

This is especially true if you think that learning television production consists primarily of mastering the equipment. But later, when facing production challenges as a professional, you will undoubtedly draw on your rigorous academic problem-solving practice, whether or not you are cognizant of your classroom training.

■ FOR THE INSTRUCTOR

Because the *Workbook* is primarily an instrument for testing, it is not always embraced by students who may feel that their time is better spent running around capturing exciting video. Underlying such an attitude is often a justified test-anxiety. To minimize or even eliminate such a mindset, you may try using the *Workbook* as a diagnostic tool, choosing not to grade the results but simply make students aware of what they have yet to learn. The initial resistance to the *Workbook* quickly dissipates when even the more experienced students realize that they still have some brushing up to do and that the course offers the opportunity to overcome their deficiencies. You could also have students complete part of the *Workbook* problems at the beginning of each classroom period. In any case, you should encourage students to solve the assigned *Workbook* problems at least initially without the aid of the *Handbook.*

The chapters in this edition of the *Workbook* correspond to those of the *Television Production Handbook,* Eleventh Edition, without necessarily being tied to them. You can assign them in the chapter order you use for the *Handbook* or any other order if more convenient or effective.

To expedite scoring the assignments in the *Workbook,* filling in bubbles substitutes for handwritten answers. Although this binary method may confine some students' urge to express themselves creatively, it greatly facilitates evaluation and, more importantly, enables you to compare the standardized scores. The *Instructor's Manual with Answer Key to Workbook,* available both in print and online, suggests ways of managing the bubble answers most efficiently.

The problem-solving applications are intended for classroom discussion, but you can also assign them as homework.

If you are using *Zettl's VideoLab* DVD-ROM, its various modules dovetail smoothly with the *Workbook* exercises. For example, you can use the disc to demonstrate some motion concepts that are impossible to properly show in the main text or the *Workbook,* such as the reversal of motion vectors when crossing the line.

Both releases of this Windows- and Mac-compatible DVD-ROM—3.0 and the new 4.0—give students virtual hands-on practice and a proven shortcut from reading about production techniques to actually applying them in the studio and in the field. The in-text ZVL cues in the *Handbook* work with both *Zettl's VideoLab 3.0* and *4.0.* The new 4.0 release incorporates additional advanced exercises.

Finally, you may want to remind your students that they have chosen your class precisely because they want to go beyond simple equipment skills—to move from gifted amateur to creative and responsible professional, from somebody who conveniently submits to the industry routines to one who innovates new and more effective ways of communicating significant ideas to media consumers.

To access additional course materials and companion resources, please visit *www .cengagebrain.com.* At the CengageBrain.com home page, search for the ISBN of the *Television Production Handbook* (from the back cover of the book), using the search box at the top of the page. This will take you to the product page, where free companion resources can be found.

■ ACKNOWLEDGMENTS

The people at Wadsworth Cengage Learning deserve much praise for managing the publication of the *Television Production Workbook,* Eleventh Edition: Michael Rosenberg, publisher; Megan Garvey, development editor; and Erin Pass, assistant editor.

I was privileged to work, once again, with my proven A-team of experts: Gary Palmatier of Ideas to Images, art director and project manager; Elizabeth von Radics, copy editor; and Ed Aiona, photographer. Not only are they exceptionally gifted professionals who can create a book from manuscript fragments and scribbles but they also draw on their competency in video and the photographic arts. Best of all, they are fun to work with.

As with previous editions, I am especially indebted to my former colleagues: Hamid Khani, Marty Gonzales, Winston Tharp, all of San Francisco State University, and Paul Rose of Utah University. They were always ready to help in a variety of ways. Thanks also to my students who contributed significantly, however unknowingly, to my formulating the various problems. The many students who doubled as on-camera talent deserve special praise.

Finally, I owe a big thank-you to my wife, Erika, who as a longtime classroom teacher, administrator, and educational consultant helped with translating the more complicated problems into a binary format that enables students to give the answers by filling in bubbles.

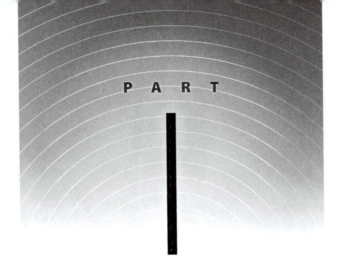

PART

I

Introduction:
Process and System

© 2012 Wadsworth, Cengage Learning

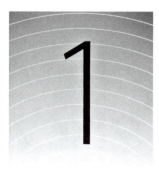

The Television Production Process

REVIEW OF KEY TERMS

Match each term with its appropriate definition by filling in the corresponding bubble.

1. **medium requirements**
2. **EFP**
3. **nonlinear editing**
4. **preproduction**
5. **effect-to-cause model**
6. **television system**
7. **technical personnel**
8. **production**
9. **linear editing**
10. **ENG**
11. **process message**
12. **postproduction**

A. The people, content, and production elements needed to generate the desired viewer effect

A
○ 1 ○ 2 ○ 3 ○ 4
○ 5 ○ 6 ○ 7 ○ 8
○ 9 ○ 10 ○ 11 ○ 12

B. Television production that covers daily events and is usually transmitted live or after immediate postproduction

B
○ 1 ○ 2 ○ 3 ○ 4
○ 5 ○ 6 ○ 7 ○ 8
○ 9 ○ 10 ○ 11 ○ 12

C. Video and audio editing phase

C
○ 1 ○ 2 ○ 3 ○ 4
○ 5 ○ 6 ○ 7 ○ 8
○ 9 ○ 10 ○ 11 ○ 12

PAGE
TOTAL

© 2012 Wadsworth, Cengage Learning

1. medium requirements	5. effect-to-cause model	9. linear editing
2. EFP	6. television system	10. ENG
3. nonlinear editing	7. technical personnel	11. process message
4. preproduction	8. production	12. postproduction

D. People who primarily operate television equipment

D
○ ○ ○ ○
1 2 3 4
○ ○ ○ ○
5 6 7 8
○ ○ ○ ○
9 10 11 12

E. Analog or digital editing that uses tape-based systems

E
○ ○ ○ ○
1 2 3 4
○ ○ ○ ○
5 6 7 8
○ ○ ○ ○
9 10 11 12

F. Allows random access to, and flexible sequencing of, recorded video and audio material

F
○ ○ ○ ○
1 2 3 4
○ ○ ○ ○
5 6 7 8
○ ○ ○ ○
9 10 11 12

G. Preparation of all production details

G
○ ○ ○ ○
1 2 3 4
○ ○ ○ ○
5 6 7 8
○ ○ ○ ○
9 10 11 12

H. The information that the viewer actually receives

H
○ ○ ○ ○
1 2 3 4
○ ○ ○ ○
5 6 7 8
○ ○ ○ ○
9 10 11 12

P A G E
T O T A L

© 2012 Wadsworth, Cengage Learning

I. All activities during the recording or televising of an event

I ○ ○ ○ ○
  1   2   3   4
○ ○ ○ ○
5   6   7   8
○ ○ ○ ○
9   10   11   12

J. The basic equipment necessary to produce video and audio signals and reconvert them into pictures and sound

J ○ ○ ○ ○
  1   2   3   4
○ ○ ○ ○
5   6   7   8
○ ○ ○ ○
9   10   11   12

K. Moving from the idea to the program objective, then backing up to the specific medium requirements to produce this objective

K ○ ○ ○ ○
  1   2   3   4
○ ○ ○ ○
5   6   7   8
○ ○ ○ ○
9   10   11   12

L. A relatively uncomplicated field production shot for postproduction

L ○ ○ ○ ○
  1   2   3   4
○ ○ ○ ○
5   6   7   8
○ ○ ○ ○
9   10   11   12

PAGE TOTAL [ ]

SECTION TOTAL [ ]

© 2012 Wadsworth, Cengage Learning

REVIEW OF EFFECT-TO-CAUSE MODEL

Select the correct answers and fill in the bubbles with the corresponding numbers.

1. Identify each part of the effect-to-cause diagram below and fill in the bubbles with the corresponding numbers.

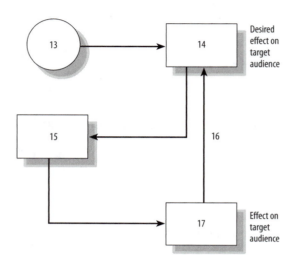

a. program content, people, and production elements

b. defined process message

c. initial idea

d. feedback

e. actual process message

1a ◯ ◯ ◯ ◯ ◯
   13 14 15 16 17

1b ◯ ◯ ◯ ◯ ◯
   13 14 15 16 17

1c ◯ ◯ ◯ ◯ ◯
   13 14 15 16 17

1d ◯ ◯ ◯ ◯ ◯
   13 14 15 16 17

1e ◯ ◯ ◯ ◯ ◯
   13 14 15 16 17

PAGE
TOTAL

© 2012 Wadsworth, Cengage Learning

2. The effect-to-cause model is especially helpful in (18) *preproduction* (19) *production* (20) *postproduction.*

| 2 | ○ 18 | ○ 19 | ○ 20 |

3. The effect-to-cause model is especially useful in the production of (21) *breaking news stories* (22) *documentaries* (23) *dramas.*

| 3 | ○ 21 | ○ 22 | ○ 23 |

4. The most important initial step in the effect-to-cause approach is (24) *determining the medium requirements* (25) *determining the available production equipment* (26) *defining the process message.*

| 4 | ○ 24 | ○ 25 | ○ 26 |

5. Feedback helps determine (27) *whether the production was efficient* (28) *how close the actual effect came to the process message* (29) *how close the actual effect came to the original idea.*

| 5 | ○ 27 | ○ 28 | ○ 29 |

6. The medium requirements include (30) *equipment and people* (31) *equipment but not people.*

| 6 | ○ 30 | ○ 31 |

7. The angle will define the (32) *process message* (33) *basic production approach* (34) *position of the camera.*

| 7 | ○ 32 | ○ 33 | ○ 34 |

8. A defined process message must contain at least the (35) *target audience* (36) *medium requirements* (37) *desired effect on the viewer.*

| 8 | ○ 35 | ○ 36 | ○ 37 |

9. Medium requirements are basically determined by the (38) *chief engineer* (39) *available equipment* (40) *process message.*

| 9 | ○ 38 | ○ 39 | ○ 40 |

10. In the effect-to-cause model, we move from (41) *idea to medium requirements to production* (42) *idea to production to process message* (43) *idea to process message to medium requirements.*

| 10 | ○ 41 | ○ 42 | ○ 43 |

PAGE TOTAL ☐

SECTION TOTAL ☐

© 2012 Wadsworth, Cengage Learning

REVIEW OF PRODUCTION PERSONNEL

1. Match each job title with the most appropriate function by filling in the corresponding bubble.

   (44) director   (48) VR operator   (51) floor manager
   (45) PA   (49) LD   (52) DP
   (46) AD   (50) producer   (53) TD
   (47) VJ

   a. In charge of all production activities on the production day

   1a ○ ○ ○ ○ ○
       44 45 46 47 48
       ○ ○ ○ ○ ○
       49 50 51 52 53

   b. In EFP, works the camera; in cinema, is in charge of the lighting and film exposure

   1b ○ ○ ○ ○ ○
       44 45 46 47 48
       ○ ○ ○ ○ ○
       49 50 51 52 53

   c. In charge of lighting

   1c ○ ○ ○ ○ ○
       44 45 46 47 48
       ○ ○ ○ ○ ○
       49 50 51 52 53

   d. Supports the director in directing activities

   1d ○ ○ ○ ○ ○
       44 45 46 47 48
       ○ ○ ○ ○ ○
       49 50 51 52 53

   e. In charge of video recording

   1e ○ ○ ○ ○ ○
       44 45 46 47 48
       ○ ○ ○ ○ ○
       49 50 51 52 53

   f. In charge of all preproduction activities

   1f ○ ○ ○ ○ ○
       44 45 46 47 48
       ○ ○ ○ ○ ○
       49 50 51 52 53

   g. Relays the director's messages to talent

   1g ○ ○ ○ ○ ○
       44 45 46 47 48
       ○ ○ ○ ○ ○
       49 50 51 52 53

   PAGE TOTAL [   ]

© 2012 Wadsworth, Cengage Learning

h. Shoots and edits own news footage

1h
( ) ( ) ( ) ( ) ( )
44 45 46 47 48
( ) ( ) ( ) ( ) ( )
49 50 51 52 53

i. In charge of a crew; usually does the switching

1i
( ) ( ) ( ) ( ) ( )
44 45 46 47 48
( ) ( ) ( ) ( ) ( )
49 50 51 52 53

j. Assists producer and director in all production phases

1j
( ) ( ) ( ) ( ) ( )
44 45 46 47 48
( ) ( ) ( ) ( ) ( )
49 50 51 52 53

2. Match each title of news personnel with its appropriate definition by filling in the corresponding bubble.

(54) writer (57) news director (60) videographer/shooter
(55) sportscaster (58) reporter (61) anchor
(56) news producer (59) assignment editor (62) VJ

a. Prepares on-the-air copy for the anchorpersons

2a
( ) ( ) ( ) ( ) ( )
54 55 56 57 58
( ) ( ) ( ) ( )
59 60 61 62

b. Responsible for all the news operations

2b
( ) ( ) ( ) ( ) ( )
54 55 56 57 58
( ) ( ) ( ) ( )
59 60 61 62

c. Combines in a single person the camera operator, the editor, the writer, and sometimes even the on-camera talent in news gathering.

2c
( ) ( ) ( ) ( ) ( )
54 55 56 57 58
( ) ( ) ( ) ( )
59 60 61 62

d. Sends reporters and videographers to specific events

2d
( ) ( ) ( ) ( ) ( )
54 55 56 57 58
( ) ( ) ( ) ( )
59 60 61 62

e. Principal presenter of newscast, normally from a studio set

2e
( ) ( ) ( ) ( ) ( )
54 55 56 57 58
( ) ( ) ( ) ( )
59 60 61 62

PAGE
TOTAL [   ]

© 2012 Wadsworth, Cengage Learning

(54) writer	(57) news director	(60) videographer/shooter
(55) sportscaster	(58) reporter	(61) anchor
(56) news producer	(59) assignment editor	(62) VJ

f. Operates camcorder and, in the absence of a reporter, decides what part of the event to cover

2f ○ ○ ○ ○ ○
54 55 56 57 58
○ ○ ○ ○
59 60 61 62

g. Gathers the news stories and often reports on-camera from the field

2g ○ ○ ○ ○ ○
54 55 56 57 58
○ ○ ○ ○
59 60 61 62

h. Responsible for individual news stories for on-the-air use

2h ○ ○ ○ ○ ○
54 55 56 57 58
○ ○ ○ ○
59 60 61 62

i. On-camera talent, giving sports content

2i ○ ○ ○ ○ ○
54 55 56 57 58
○ ○ ○ ○
59 60 61 62

PAGE TOTAL

SECTION TOTAL

© 2012 Wadsworth, Cengage Learning

REVIEW OF TECHNICAL SYSTEMS

1. Identify each of the major elements of the basic television system by filling in the corresponding bubble.

a. audio signal   **d.** TV receiver sound   **f.** VR

b. microphone   **e.** TV receiver image   **g.** TV camera

c. video signal

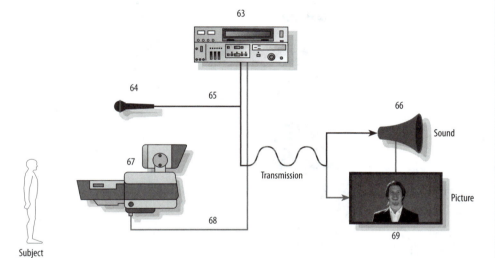

1a ○ ○ ○ ○
    63 64 65 66
    ○ ○ ○
    67 68 69

1b ○ ○ ○ ○
    63 64 65 66
    ○ ○ ○
    67 68 69

1c ○ ○ ○ ○
    63 64 65 66
    ○ ○ ○
    67 68 69

1d ○ ○ ○ ○
    63 64 65 66
    ○ ○ ○
    67 68 69

1e ○ ○ ○ ○
    63 64 65 66
    ○ ○ ○
    67 68 69

1f ○ ○ ○ ○
    63 64 65 66
    ○ ○ ○
    67 68 69

1g ○ ○ ○ ○
    63 64 65 66
    ○ ○ ○
    67 68 69

P A G E
T O T A L [   ]

PHOTO: EDWARD AIONA

© 2012 Wadsworth, Cengage Learning

2. Identify each major component of the expanded television system by filling in the corresponding bubble.

a. cameras 1 and 2

b. transmitter

c. preview monitors

d. video switcher

e. home TV receiver

f. audio console

g. video recorder

h. line monitor

i. CCUs 1 and 2

j. audio monitor speaker

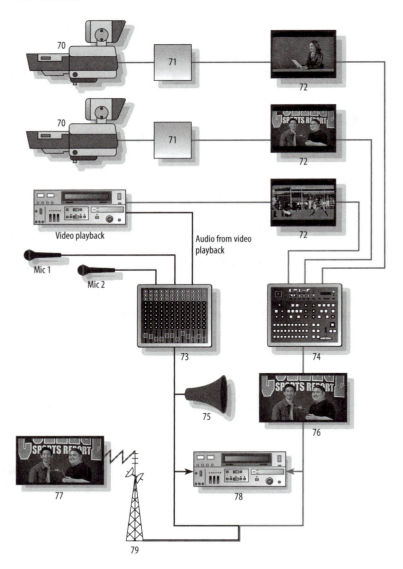

Video playback

Mic 1

Mic 2

Audio from video playback

2a 70 71 72 73 74   75 76 77 78 79

2b 70 71 72 73 74   75 76 77 78 79

2c 70 71 72 73 74   75 76 77 78 79

2d 70 71 72 73 74   75 76 77 78 79

2e 70 71 72 73 74   75 76 77 78 79

2f 70 71 72 73 74   75 76 77 78 79

2g 70 71 72 73 74   75 76 77 78 79

2h 70 71 72 73 74   75 76 77 78 79

2i 70 71 72 73 74   75 76 77 78 79

2j 70 71 72 73 74   75 76 77 78 79

P A G E
T O T A L

PHOTOS: EDWARD AIONA

© 2012 Wadsworth, Cengage Learning

3. Match each system element with its appropriate function by filling in the corresponding bubble.

(80) cameras
(81) preview monitors
(82) TV receiver
(83) audio monitor speaker
(84) line monitor

(85) microphones
(86) switcher
(87) audio console
(88) CCUs
(89) VR

a. To record video and audio signals on recording media

3a ○ ○ ○ ○ ○
      80 81 82 83 84
      ○ ○ ○ ○ ○
      85 86 87 88 89

b. To control the picture quality of the television cameras

3b ○ ○ ○ ○ ○
      80 81 82 83 84
      ○ ○ ○ ○ ○
      85 86 87 88 89

c. To translate the broadcast signals into pictures and sound

3c ○ ○ ○ ○ ○
      80 81 82 83 84
      ○ ○ ○ ○ ○
      85 86 87 88 89

d. To convert what we hear into electrical signals

3d ○ ○ ○ ○ ○
      80 81 82 83 84
      ○ ○ ○ ○ ○
      85 86 87 88 89

e. To control the audio quality of the various audio inputs

3e ○ ○ ○ ○ ○
      80 81 82 83 84
      ○ ○ ○ ○ ○
      85 86 87 88 89

f. To convert what the lens sees into electrical signals

3f ○ ○ ○ ○ ○
      80 81 82 83 84
      ○ ○ ○ ○ ○
      85 86 87 88 89

g. To select video inputs

3g ○ ○ ○ ○ ○
      80 81 82 83 84
      ○ ○ ○ ○ ○
      85 86 87 88 89

PAGE TOTAL [   ]

© 2012 Wadsworth, Cengage Learning

(80) cameras	(85) microphones
(81) preview monitors	(86) switcher
(82) TV receiver	(87) audio console
(83) audio monitor speaker	(88) CCUs
(84) line monitor	(89) VR

h. To display the pictures supplied by the various video sources

3h ○ ○ ○ ○ ○
    80 81 82 83 84
    ○ ○ ○ ○ ○
    85 86 87 88 89

i. To display the line-out pictures

3i ○ ○ ○ ○ ○
    80 81 82 83 84
    ○ ○ ○ ○ ○
    85 86 87 88 89

j. To reproduce the line-out sound

3j ○ ○ ○ ○ ○
    80 81 82 83 84
    ○ ○ ○ ○ ○
    85 86 87 88 89

PAGE TOTAL

SECTION TOTAL

© 2012 Wadsworth, Cengage Learning

REVIEW QUIZ

*Mark the following statements as true or false by filling in the bubbles in the **T** (for true) or **F** (for false) column.*

	T	F

1. The switcher does not allow for instantaneous editing.

2. In the television studio, we use spotlights and floodlights.

3. Digital memory devices (memory cards) can be used to record video segments.

4. The primary function of the C.G. is to enhance picture quality.

5. A microphone converts sound into digital video.

6. Linear editing involves copying shots onto another videotape in a specific order.

7. At least two VRs are needed for linear postproduction editing.

8. With nonlinear editing you can edit directly from the source tapes to the edit master tape.

9. All audio consoles can select the signals from multiple incoming audio sources and control sound volume.

10. A digital camcorder can use videotape as its recording media.

	T	F
1	◯ 90	◯ 91
2	◯ 92	◯ 93
3	◯ 94	◯ 95
4	◯ 96	◯ 97
5	◯ 98	◯ 99
6	◯ 100	◯ 101
7	◯ 102	◯ 103
8	◯ 104	◯ 105
9	◯ 106	◯ 107
10	◯ 108	◯ 109

SECTION TOTAL [ ]

© 2012 Wadsworth, Cengage Learning

PROBLEM-SOLVING APPLICATIONS

Think through each production problem and consider the various options. Then pick the most effective solution and justify your choice.

1. List in any order the major components (equipment) of the expanded television system that will allow you to produce and select optimal pictures from three studio cameras, produce optimal sound from four microphones, and video-record and simultaneously transmit the signals to a television receiver. Now order these components and connect them with lines that show the basic signal flow from cameras, microphones, and the various video and audio selections to the video recorder and the home television receiver.

2. List the components of a linear videotape-editing system that permits a dissolve; then draw a diagram that shows the basic signal flow for these components.

3. What system elements are incorporated into a single camcorder? What are some of the advantages and the disadvantages of the camcorder system compared with those of the expanded television system?

4. What exactly distinguishes ENG from EFP?

5. Apply the effect-to-cause model to a variety of goal-directed programs. Pay particular attention to a precise process message.

6. How does a clearly stated process message help with the medium requirements?

7. List two tapeless recording media and describe the advantages and the disadvantages of each.

© 2012 Wadsworth, Cengage Learning

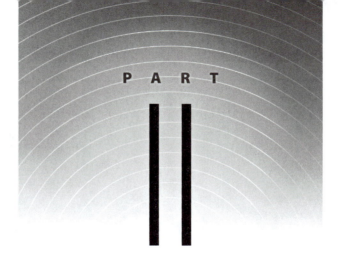

Preproduction

© 2012 Wadsworth, Cengage Learning

The Producer in Preproduction

REVIEW OF KEY TERMS

Match each term with its appropriate definition by filling in the corresponding bubble.

1. **target audience**   4. **demographics**   7. **share**
2. **program proposal**   5. **production schedule**   8. **rating**
3. **time line**   6. **psychographics**   9. **treatment**

A. A breakdown of time blocks for various activities on the actual production day

A ○ ○ ○ ○ ○
   1 2 3 4 5
   ○ ○ ○ ○
   6 7 8 9

B. Audience factors concerned with such data as consumer buying habits, values, and lifestyles

B ○ ○ ○ ○ ○
   1 2 3 4 5
   ○ ○ ○ ○
   6 7 8 9

C. Percentage of television households tuned to a specific station in relation to all HUT

C ○ ○ ○ ○ ○
   1 2 3 4 5
   ○ ○ ○ ○
   6 7 8 9

D. Percentage of television households tuned to a specific station in relation to the total number of television households

D ○ ○ ○ ○ ○
   1 2 3 4 5
   ○ ○ ○ ○
   6 7 8 9

P A G E
T O T A L   [   ]

© 2012 Wadsworth, Cengage Learning

1. target audience	4. demographics	7. share
2. program proposal	5. production schedule	8. rating
3. time line	6. psychographics	9. treatment

E. The calendar dates for preproduction, production, and postproduction activities

E ○ ○ ○ ○ ○
   1 2 3 4 5
   ○ ○ ○ ○
   6 7 8 9

F. Written document that outlines the process message and the major aspects of a television presentation

F ○ ○ ○ ○ ○
   1 2 3 4 5
   ○ ○ ○ ○
   6 7 8 9

G. Audience factors concerned with such data as age, gender, marital status, and income

G ○ ○ ○ ○ ○
   1 2 3 4 5
   ○ ○ ○ ○
   6 7 8 9

H. Narrative description of a television program

H ○ ○ ○ ○ ○
   1 2 3 4 5
   ○ ○ ○ ○
   6 7 8 9

I. Viewers identified to receive a specific message

I ○ ○ ○ ○ ○
   1 2 3 4 5
   ○ ○ ○ ○
   6 7 8 9

PAGE TOTAL ☐

SECTION TOTAL ☐

© 2012 Wadsworth, Cengage Learning

REVIEW OF PREPRODUCTION PLANNING: GENERATING IDEAS

1. Expand three of the following four clusters according to the key word. Develop a precise process message for each. Choose the key word for the fourth cluster and develop its process message accordingly.

a. cluster 1

Water conservation

Process message: _____

_____

_____

_____

_____

_____

© 2012 Wadsworth, Cengage Learning

b. cluster 2

Peace

Process message: _____
_____
_____
_____
_____
_____

© 2012 Wadsworth, Cengage Learning

c. cluster 3

Alternative
energy sources

Process message: _____

_____

_____

_____

_____

_____

© 2012 Wadsworth, Cengage Learning

d. cluster 4 (on a subject of your choice)

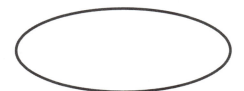

Process message: _____

_____

_____

_____

_____

_____

© 2012 Wadsworth, Cengage Learning

REVIEW OF EVALUATING IDEAS

Select the correct answers and fill in the bubbles with the corresponding numbers.

1. In the preproduction flowchart below, match the unmarked steps with the corresponding numbers.

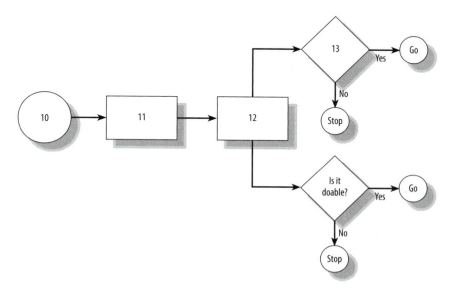

a. angle

b. idea

c. worth doing?

d. process message

1a ○ ○ ○ ○
   10 11 12 13

1b ○ ○ ○ ○
   10 11 12 13

1c ○ ○ ○ ○
   10 11 12 13

1d ○ ○ ○ ○
   10 11 12 13

SECTION
TOTAL [ ]

© 2012 Wadsworth, Cengage Learning

REVIEW OF PROGRAM PROPOSAL

Select the correct answers and fill in the bubbles with the corresponding numbers.

1. The standard program proposal usually contains a (14) *program objective* (15) *list of studio or remote equipment* (16) *detailed storyboard.*

2. A show treatment usually contains a (17) *one-page sample of the dialogue and the video and audio cues* (18) *script sample with major visualization cues* (19) *brief narrative description of what we see and hear.*

3. A well-stated process message should (20) *state the steps of moving from idea to finished show* (21) *include the specific objective of the show* (22) *describe the process of moving from idea to detailed script.*

4. A good description of the target audience should include (23) *demographic and psychographic indicators* (24) *the number of potential viewers* (25) *only demographic indicators.*

5. When preparing a budget for an outside client, you can skip the cost for (26) *the writer* (27) *the equipment* (28) *neither the writer nor the equipment.*

6. In a large production, the daily activities are supervised by the (29) *PA* (30) *executive producer* (31) *line producer.*

7. Preproduction is necessary for (32) *every production except ENG* (33) *studio productions only* (34) *EFPs only.*

8. The individual who is normally absent during the beginning stage of preproduction is the (35) *producer* (36) *chief engineer* (37) *director.*

9. In the production schedule on the facing page, identify potential problems for each EFP shoot. From the list below, select the items that best describe the problems and fill in the corresponding bubbles. Most shoots have more than one problem. *(Multiple answers are possible.)*

   (38) different talent; break in continuity

   (39) different director and crew; potential break in style and continuity

   (40) need for remote truck questionable relative to the production scope

   (41) shooting time too late; will cause lighting and continuity problems in postproduction

   (42) should be done in conjunction with similar previous activity or opening

   (43) facilities request very late

   (44) facilities request too late

   (45) too little time allotted

   (46) too much time allotted

1	◯ 14	◯ 15	◯ 16
2	◯ 17	◯ 18	◯ 19
3	◯ 20	◯ 21	◯ 22
4	◯ 23	◯ 24	◯ 25
5	◯ 26	◯ 27	◯ 28
6	◯ 29	◯ 30	◯ 31
7	◯ 32	◯ 33	◯ 34
8	◯ 35	◯ 36	◯ 37

PAGE TOTAL ▢

© 2012 Wadsworth, Cengage Learning

Show/Scene/Subject	Date/Time	Location	Facilities	Talent/Personnel
Leisure CiTy SHOOT 1 OPENING	Aug.8 8:30 am 4:30 pm	In fronT of compleTed model home— Simple opening remarks. 1:00 min.	Normal EFP as per fac. req. Aug.8	TalenT: LYNNE DirecTor: B.R. Crew A scheduled
Leisure CiTy SHOOT 2	Aug.9 12:30 pm 1:00 pm	Homes under consTrucTion. Show homes being consTrucTed.	Special remoTe Truck. See equipmenT fac. req. Aug. 8	TalenT: LYNNE DirecTor: B.R. Crew A scheduled
Leisure CiTy SHOOT 3	Aug. 10 8:30 am 9:00 am	InTerior of model home. Shows how Typical home looks and works inside.	Normal EFP as per fac. req. Aug.7	TalenT: LYNNE DirecTor: B.R. Crew A scheduled
Leisure CiTy SHOOT 4	Aug. 11 7:30 pm 10:30 pm	Homes under consTrucTion.	Normal EFP as per fac. req. Aug.11	TalenT: SUSAN DirecTor: JOHN HEWITT Crew B scheduled
Leisure CiTy SHOOT 5	Aug. 12 8:00 pm 8:30 pm	In fronT of compleTed model home— Simple closing remarks. 1:30 min.	Special remoTe Truck. See equipmenT fac. req. Aug.8	TalenT: SUSAN DirecTor: B.R. Crew A scheduled

a. shoot 1

b. shoot 2

c. shoot 3

d. shoot 4

e. shoot 5

9a ○ ○ ○ ○ ○
38 39 40 41 42
○ ○ ○ ○
43 44 45 46

9b ○ ○ ○ ○ ○
38 39 40 41 42
○ ○ ○ ○
43 44 45 46

9c ○ ○ ○ ○ ○
38 39 40 41 42
○ ○ ○ ○
43 44 45 46

9d ○ ○ ○ ○ ○
38 39 40 41 42
○ ○ ○ ○
43 44 45 46

9e ○ ○ ○ ○ ○
38 39 40 41 42
○ ○ ○ ○
43 44 45 46

PAGE TOTAL [ ]

SECTION TOTAL [ ]

© 2012 Wadsworth, Cengage Learning

REVIEW OF COORDINATION

Select the correct answers and fill in the bubbles with the corresponding numbers.

1. The person principally responsible for all preproduction communication is the
   (47) *director* (48) *producer* (49) *executive producer.*

2. When coordinating an EFP on water conservation, you don't have to include in your
   preproduction memos the (50) *technical personnel* (51) *sales manager* (52) *PA.*

3. In a typical television station, facilities requests are necessary (53) *only if you
   are planning a new production* (54) *for every production except ENG* (55) *for the
   preproduction conference.*

4. When sending your memos via e-mail, you must insist on a written response from
   (56) *production people only* (57) *technical personnel only* (58) *every person on your
   mailing list.*

5. The timeline is usually drawn up by the (59) *executive producer* (60) *producer*
   (61) *director.*

6. The production schedule is usually drawn up by the (62) *executive producer*
   (63) *producer* (64) *assistant director.*

7. A schedule change is normally communicated to the production team by the
   (65) *executive producer* (66) *producer* (67) *director.*

8. Informing the crew of the process message is the responsibility of the (68) *director*
   (69) *executive producer* (70) *chief engineer.*

1	○ 47	○ 48	○ 49
2	○ 50	○ 51	○ 52
3	○ 53	○ 54	○ 55
4	○ 56	○ 57	○ 58
5	○ 59	○ 60	○ 61
6	○ 62	○ 63	○ 64
7	○ 65	○ 66	○ 67
8	○ 68	○ 69	○ 70

SECTION TOTAL [ ]

© 2012 Wadsworth, Cengage Learning

Course No. _____ Date _____ Name _____

REVIEW OF UNIONS AND LEGAL MATTERS

Select the correct answers and fill in the bubbles with the corresponding numbers.

1. The theater department of the local high school would like to play its video production of Arthur Miller's *Death of a Salesman* on a local TV station. The student actors (71) *will* (72) *will not* need AFTRA clearance.

   1 ◯ 71   ◯ 72

2. A potential sponsor would like a treatment of one of the proposed segments of your humanities series. Sending the script instead is (73) *acceptable* (74) *not acceptable*.

   2 ◯ 73   ◯ 74

3. For each of the trade unions listed, mark whether it is a (75) *technical* or a (76) *nontechnical* union by filling in the appropriate bubble.

   a. NABET

   3a ◯ 75   ◯ 76

   b. IATSE

   3b ◯ 75   ◯ 76

   c. SEG

   3c ◯ 75   ◯ 76

   d. WGA

   3d ◯ 75   ◯ 76

   e. DGA

   3e ◯ 75   ◯ 76

   f. SAG

   3f ◯ 75   ◯ 76

   g. AFTRA

   3g ◯ 75   ◯ 76

   h. IBEW

   3h ◯ 75   ◯ 76

   i. AFM

   3i ◯ 75   ◯ 76

PAGE TOTAL [   ]

© 2012 Wadsworth, Cengage Learning

4. Determine whether each of the production cases below (77) *requires* or (78) *does not require* copyright clearance and fill in the appropriate bubble.

a. using a recent CD recording of Bach's *Toccata and Fugue in F Major* as the theme for a show on architecture

4a ○ 77 ○ 78

b. using a Beatles song as the theme for a documentary on the history of rock music

4b ○ 77 ○ 78

c. taking close-ups of paintings in your news coverage of the local outdoor art festival

4c ○ 77 ○ 78

d. using a sixteenth-century book to make a digital scan of a church floor plan for your Renaissance show

4d ○ 77 ○ 78

e. using a recently published art book to make a digital scan of a church floor plan for your show on Baroque art

4e ○ 77 ○ 78

f. using a record album cover as the background for your opening and closing titles on a music series

4f ○ 77 ○ 78

g. using three different scenes of published plays as the basis for your series about acting for the video camera

4g ○ 77 ○ 78

h. having your pianist friend play and record her own composition for use as a theme on your weekly music series

4h ○ 77 ○ 78

PAGE TOTAL

SECTION TOTAL

© 2012 Wadsworth, Cengage Learning

REVIEW OF RATINGS

Select the correct answers and fill in the bubbles with the corresponding numbers.

1. HUT is a factor in figuring (79) *shares* (80) *ratings*.

2. A rating of 13 indicates that (81) *13 of 2,000* (82) *800 of 6,000* (83) *13 of 1,300* (84) *total television households* (85) *of all households using television* are tuned to your station. **(Fill in two bubbles.)**

3. A share of 22 means that (86) *175 of 2,200* (87) *22 of 2,200* (88) *175 of 800* (89) *total television households* (90) *of all households using television* are tuned to your station. **(Fill in two bubbles.)**

4. All rating services use (91) *audience samples* (92) *total populations* as a basis for their figures.

5. Share figures are usually (93) *higher* (94) *lower* than rating figures.

1 ◯ 79   ◯ 80

2 ◯ 81   ◯ 82   ◯ 83
   ◯ 84   ◯ 85

3 ◯ 86   ◯ 87   ◯ 88
   ◯ 89   ◯ 90

4 ◯ 91   ◯ 92

5 ◯ 93   ◯ 94

SECTION
TOTAL [   ]

© 2012 Wadsworth, Cengage Learning

REVIEW QUIZ

*Mark the following statements as true or false by filling in the bubbles in the **T** (for true) or
F (for false) column.*

		T	F
1.	Normally, it is the writer who establishes the initial production process.	1 ○ 95	○ 96
2.	The facilities request for a specific production should contain equipment and technical facilities.	2 ○ 97	○ 98
3.	The two major criteria for evaluating program ideas are *Is it doable?* and *How much does it cost?*	3 ○ 99	○ 100
4.	A show treatment is necessary only for television documentaries.	4 ○ 101	○ 102
5.	CDs sold in record stores are in the public domain, so you can use them for television productions without securing copyright clearance.	5 ○ 103	○ 104
6.	Budgets must include expenses for preproduction, production, and all postproduction activities as well as personnel.	6 ○ 105	○ 106
7.	Whereas the budget is essential for a program proposal, a description of the target audience is not.	7 ○ 107	○ 108
8.	Broadcast unions include technical personnel only.	8 ○ 109	○ 110
9.	Demographic descriptors help define the target audience.	9 ○ 111	○ 112
10.	Once you have generated a worthwhile message, the producer can leave the day-to-day production details to the PA.	10 ○ 113	○ 114
11.	The producer works only with nontechnical personnel.	11 ○ 115	○ 116
12.	Because production is primarily a creative activity, any type of production system would prove counterproductive.	12 ○ 117	○ 118
13.	The line producer is responsible primarily for budgets.	13 ○ 119	○ 120
14.	A time line and a production schedule are the same thing.	14 ○ 121	○ 122
15.	Two of the important items in an effective program proposal are a treatment and a description of the target audience.	15 ○ 123	○ 124

SECTION TOTAL [ ]

© 2012 Wadsworth, Cengage Learning

PROBLEM-SOLVING APPLICATIONS

1. The art director asks you, the producer, whether her floor plan will allow optimal camera traffic. Are you the right person to answer this question? If so, why? If not, who would be the appropriate person to answer this question?

2. Your new comedy series is shot multicamera-style in the studio. You intend to video-record the dress rehearsal and the uninterrupted live-recorded show for later on-air scheduling. The production manager suggests that you prepare a budget that includes a generous amount of money for postproduction editing. Do you agree with the production manager? If so, why? If not, why not?

3. Write an effective program proposal for one or more of the following ideas. The proposal should include these points: (1) program title, (2) target audience, (3) process message (objective), (4) show treatment, (5) ideal program time and broadcast or other distribution channel, and (6) tentative budget.

   a. a series of shows about the effects of television on children

   b. a weekly fashion show

   c. a 10-week series about how to preserve water

   d. a three-show series about your favorite sport

   e. a five-show series for seventh- and eighth-graders about the dangers of drugs

   f. a 10-part series about human dignity and happiness

   g. a 5-part mini-documentary series about road rage and safe driving

   h. a 10-part series about the life and the work of a classical composer or a contemporary rock musician

   i. a 10-part series about the life and the work of your favorite sports figure

4. The local high-school video club has produced a music video, using magazine pictures that are synchronized with the latest recording of a rock band. The students plead with you to persuade the local cable company to put it on the air. What concerns, if any, do you have about airing this video recording? What can you do to accommodate the group's request?

5. The art director claims that she never received the director's e-mail about a set for the upcoming studio show of a dance recital. What simple steps would you suggest to remedy such problems?

© 2012 Wadsworth, Cengage Learning

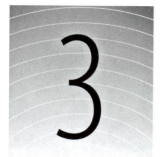

The Script

REVIEW OF KEY TERMS

Match each term with its appropriate definition by filling in the corresponding bubble.

1. partial two-column A/V script
2. event order
3. goal-directed information
4. two-column A/V script
5. classical dramaturgy
6. show format
7. single-column drama script
8. fact sheet

A. Lists the items that have to be shown on-camera and their main features

A ○ ○ ○ ○
    1 2 3 4
   ○ ○ ○ ○
    5 6 7 8

B. Used to describe a show for which the dialogue is indicated but not completely written out

B ○ ○ ○ ○
    1 2 3 4
   ○ ○ ○ ○
    5 6 7 8

C. Program content intended to be learned by viewers

C ○ ○ ○ ○
    1 2 3 4
   ○ ○ ○ ○
    5 6 7 8

D. A list of routine show segments

D ○ ○ ○ ○
    1 2 3 4
   ○ ○ ○ ○
    5 6 7 8

PAGE TOTAL ☐

© 2012 Wadsworth, Cengage Learning

1. partial two-column A/V script	3. goal-directed information	6. show format	
2. event order	4. two-column A/V script	7. single-column drama script	
	5. classical dramaturgy	8. fact sheet	

E. The lineup of event details

E ○ ○ ○ ○
  1 2 3 4
○ ○ ○ ○
  5 6 7 8

F. Traditional format for dramatic television and motion pictures scripts

F ○ ○ ○ ○
  1 2 3 4
○ ○ ○ ○
  5 6 7 8

G. Traditional script with audio information in the right column and video information in the left

G ○ ○ ○ ○
  1 2 3 4
○ ○ ○ ○
  5 6 7 8

H. Traditional composition of a play

H ○ ○ ○ ○
  1 2 3 4
○ ○ ○ ○
  5 6 7 8

PAGE TOTAL

SECTION TOTAL

© 2012 Wadsworth, Cengage Learning

REVIEW OF BASIC SCRIPT FORMATS

Select the correct answers and fill in the bubbles with the corresponding numbers.

1. Each of the following three figures (**a** through **c**) shows a script segment that contains some format errors. For each figure identify the specific format errors: (9) *unnecessary talent instructions* (10) *video or audio instructions in wrong column* (11) *incomplete dialogue* (12) *unnecessary camera instructions* (13) *nonessential and confusing information.* **(Multiple answers are possible.)**

   a. fully scripted serial drama (excerpt only)

   1a ◯ ◯ ◯ ◯ ◯
       9 10 11 12 13

GARY'S OFFICE: DAY

GARY is working intensely at his computer and ignores two telephone calls, when KIM bursts cheerfully into his office.

CUT TO CAMERA 3 WHEN KIM ENTERS

               KIM

           Let's go for coffee.

        GARY (not looking up)

           Don't have time.

               KIM

        Oh, shucks, make time.

              GARY

    You seem to be in a good mood today.

               KIM

     I'm always in a good mood…

              GARY

  [Says something about having to finish the report]

               KIM

[Tries to persuade GARY to pay more attention to her]

CUE GARY TO STAND UP AND CUT TO CAMERA 1 WHEN HE GETS UP

© 2012 Wadsworth, Cengage Learning

b. standard A/V script of brief feature story on the value of books (excerpt only)

Agency	Hot Stuff	Writer	Mary Smart
Client	Papermill Creek Publishing	Producer	Maurice Smart
Project	Book Promotion	Director	Chul Heo
Title	Books Are Alive!	Art Director	Buzz Palmer
Subject		Medium	EFP HDTV
Job #	011	Contact	Smart
Code #	HZWB11	Draft	2

VIDEO	AUDIO
CU Becky Take camera 3	BECKY: No, books are certainly not dead. On the contrary, 20 percent more books were printed worldwide last year than in any previous year.
Fade in sound of printing presses	Cue Becky to go to bookcase and look at some books.
CU of Peter. Must look annoyed.	PETER: [Says something about digital storage being so much better than clumsy books.]
Sound of books being dropped	BECKY: CU of her dropping books. Well, I think you are an ignorant nerd. How many books do you own? PETER: None!
Sound of Becky laughing	

PAGE TOTAL

© 2012 Wadsworth, Cengage Learning

c. fact sheet

1c ○ ○ ○ ○ ○
9 10 11 12 13

SHOW: Tech News

DATE: Aug. 20

HOST: Larry W.

PROPS: New Extreme Printer (operational)

1. New super color laser printer.

2. Medium shot of open printer. Zoom in on ink cartridges. Prints are permanent. Will outlast Grandma's chemical photos.

3. Pan right to operating panel. Easy, intuitive operation. Just follow the instructions.

4. CU of operation manual.

5. CU of Larry:

LARRY: Let's do some printing right now and see how easy it is.

[Larry plugs printer into his laptop.]

Larry [looks enthusiastic]: As you can see, all I needed to do is access the picture on my laptop and click the Print command.

6. And it is quiet. [Larry cups his ears.]

7. Extreme close-up of Larry.

LARRY: Be sure to take advantage of our introductory offer. But hurry! This once-in-a-lifetime opportunity expires on Thursday.

GO TO BLACK

PAGE TOTAL

SECTION TOTAL

© 2012 Wadsworth, Cengage Learning

REVIEW OF STORY STRUCTURE, CONFLICT, AND DRAMATURGY

Select the correct answers and fill in the bubbles with the corresponding numbers.

1. Select the most common four elements of the basic dramatic story structure: (14) *theme, plot, story, characters* (15) *theme, plot, characters, environment* (16) *plot, characters, action, environment.*

1 ◯ ◯ ◯
   14   15   16

2. Read the following very brief treatment excerpts and indicate whether the conflicts are (17) *plot-based* or (18) *character-based.*

a. A drunk driver goes through a stoplight and hits a car in the intersection. By chance both drivers end up in the same emergency room. They begin discussing the physical danger of driving under the influence. The discussion turns into an argument. One of the drivers crawls out of bed and tries to hit the other one. The nurse stops the fight just in time.

2a ◯ ◯
   17   18

b. A young doctor, who has been fascinated with Africa since elementary school, decides to switch from being a successful family care provider to an AIDS researcher at a San Francisco clinic. She finally can't bear the slow progress in the lab any longer and decides to make her first Africa trip to help stem the AIDS epidemic in Zwamumbu [fictitious name]. With the help of an international relief organization, she opens a clinic and, within a short time, has gained the respect and the love of hundreds of adults and children for the "miracles" she performs as a doctor. But during a political uprising of a neighboring warlord, the clinic is invaded and she is accidentally shot in the crossfire.

2b ◯ ◯
   17   18

c. A young doctor is summoned by a world health organization to deliver AIDS medicine to a Zwamumbu international health clinic. This is a high-risk mission because the president of Zwamumbu has prohibited any use of AIDS medication. His justification is one of denial. In his words: "We do not have AIDS in our country." After several scary moments, such as the search at airport customs, the doctor not only manages to deliver the medicine but also helps administer it to the children who are already HIV infected. The president's secret service people learn about her activity and get permission to assassinate her. Despite tight security at the clinic, the order is carried out successfully. Posing as an AIDS patient, the assassin confronts the young doctor and, repeating the president's statement, shoots her.

2c ◯ ◯
   17   18

PAGE TOTAL ☐

© 2012 Wadsworth, Cengage Learning

3. Fill in the bubbles whose numbers correspond with the numbers in the diagram below, identifying the various principal developmental steps of a classical dramaturgy.

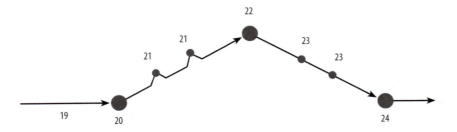

a. point of attack

b. climax

c. resolution

d. falling action and consequences of major crisis

e. exposition

f. rising action and additional conflicts

3a	○ 19	○ 20	○ 21
	○ 22	○ 23	○ 24
3b	○ 19	○ 20	○ 21
	○ 22	○ 23	○ 24
3c	○ 19	○ 20	○ 21
	○ 22	○ 23	○ 24
3d	○ 19	○ 20	○ 21
	○ 22	○ 23	○ 24
3e	○ 19	○ 20	○ 21
	○ 22	○ 23	○ 24
3f	○ 19	○ 20	○ 21
	○ 22	○ 23	○ 24

PAGE TOTAL _____

SECTION TOTAL _____

© 2012 Wadsworth, Cengage Learning

REVIEW QUIZ

Mark the following statements as true or false by filling in the bubbles in the **T** (for true) or **F** (for false) column.

1. In the resolution phase, the hero is always condemned.

2. The fact sheet and the show format have identical script formats.

3. The process message is especially useful for programs that contain primarily goal-directed information.

4. In a goal-directed program, the basic idea should lead to a precise process message.

5. The difference between a standard two-column A/V script format and a partial two-column A/V script is that the latter contains no video information.

6. In a classical dramaturgy, the point of attack marks the first major crisis.

7. The from-outside-in plots are primarily character-based.

8. A plot can develop from outside-in or from inside-out.

9. The rising as well as the falling action can include a number of crises.

10. The script is an effective communication device for all three production phases.

11. The standard two-column A/V script shows the video information on the left side and the audio information on the right.

	T	F
1	25	26
2	27	28
3	29	30
4	31	32
5	33	34
6	35	36
7	37	38
8	39	40
9	41	42
10	43	44
11	45	46

SECTION TOTAL

© 2012 Wadsworth, Cengage Learning

PROBLEM-SOLVING APPLICATIONS

1. Analyze three or four programs of a dramatic crime series and see whether the conflicts are primarily character-based, plot-based, or both. Justify your analyses.

2. How can you use plot to develop character?

3. Write a treatment of a one-hour special that includes all six elements of the classical dramaturgy.

4. Analyze a single program of a dramatic or comedy series and list all situations (verbal or action) that create an obvious conflict.

© 2012 Wadsworth, Cengage Learning

The Director in Preproduction

REVIEW OF KEY TERMS

Match each term with its appropriate definition by filling in the corresponding bubble.

1. time line
2. process message
3. facilities request

4. locking-in
5. sequencing
6. medium requirements

7. visualization
8. storyboard
9. production schedule

A. A series of sketches of the key shots

A	○ ○ ○ ○ ○
	1 2 3 4 5
	○ ○ ○ ○
	6 7 8 9

B. All content elements, production elements, and people needed to generate the defined process message

B	○ ○ ○ ○ ○
	1 2 3 4 5
	○ ○ ○ ○
	6 7 8 9

C. The control and the structuring of a series of shots during editing

C	○ ○ ○ ○ ○
	1 2 3 4 5
	○ ○ ○ ○
	6 7 8 9

D. An especially vivid mental image—visual or aural—during script analysis that determines the subsequent visualizations and sequencing

D	○ ○ ○ ○ ○
	1 2 3 4 5
	○ ○ ○ ○
	6 7 8 9

PAGE
TOTAL

© 2012 Wadsworth, Cengage Learning

1. time line	4. locking-in	7. visualization
2. process message	5. sequencing	8. storyboard
3. facilities request	6. medium requirements	9. production schedule

E. The mental image of a shot or several key images of a sequence

E
○ ○ ○ ○ ○
1　2　3　4　5
○ ○ ○ ○
6　7　8　9

F. The calendar that shows the preproduction, production, and postproduction dates and who is doing what, when, and where

F
○ ○ ○ ○ ○
1　2　3　4　5
○ ○ ○ ○
6　7　8　9

G. The message actually received by the viewer while watching a television program

G
○ ○ ○ ○ ○
1　2　3　4　5
○ ○ ○ ○
6　7　8　9

H. A list that contains all technical facilities needed for a specific production

H
○ ○ ○ ○ ○
1　2　3　4　5
○ ○ ○ ○
6　7　8　9

I. A breakdown of time blocks for various activities on the actual production day

I
○ ○ ○ ○ ○
1　2　3　4　5
○ ○ ○ ○
6　7　8　9

PAGE TOTAL

SECTION TOTAL

© 2012 Wadsworth, Cengage Learning

REVIEW OF PROCESS MESSAGE AND PRODUCTION METHOD

1. Evaluate to what extent the following four process messages will (10) *help* (11) *not help* you visualize key show elements and provide (12) *clear* (13) *only very few or no* clues to the various medium requirements. ***(Fill in two bubbles.)***

a. The program should show racecar drivers.

1a	○ 10	○ 11
	○ 12	○ 13

b. The program should make non–sports viewers admire, if not feel, the ballet-like skills of basketball players.

1b	○ 10	○ 11
	○ 12	○ 13

c. The program should make people drive better.

1c	○ 10	○ 11
	○ 12	○ 13

d. The program should show five different ways a family can save water during their morning shower and grooming.

1d	○ 10	○ 11
	○ 12	○ 13

e. The program should demonstrate to the target audience (daily commuters) the benefits of turn signals and the consequences of ignoring them in rush-hour traffic.

1e	○ 10	○ 11
	○ 12	○ 13

f. The program should help people save water.

1f	○ 10	○ 11
	○ 12	○ 13

g. This program is a series of comedy shows.

1g	○ 10	○ 11
	○ 12	○ 13

h. The program should help children learn about safety when walking to school.

1h	○ 10	○ 11
	○ 12	○ 13

PAGE TOTAL

...ngage Learning

2. A valuable process message should include (14) *a specific audience* (15) *specific production equipment* (16) *the intended effect on the audience.* **(Multiple answers are possible.)**

2	○ 14	○ 15	○ 16

3. The translation of process message to video images is greatly aided by (17) *location scouting* (18) *a storyboard* (19) *a floor plan.*

3	○ 17	○ 18	○ 19

4. Process message 1e suggests (20) *a series of location EFPs for extensive postproduction* (21) *a studio show* (22) *a single half-hour field pickup during which a videographer is riding with a highway patrol officer in rush-hour traffic.*

4	○ 20	○ 21	○ 22

5. Look at process message 1b. It suggests (23) *a recorded live pickup of a professional basketball game* (24) *an EFP with staged plays on the basketball court* (25) *a live game restaged in the studio.*

5	○ 23	○ 24	○ 25

PAGE TOTAL [ ]

SECTION TOTAL [ ]

© 2012 Wadsworth, Cengage Learning

REVIEW OF SCRIPT MARKING

1. Match each field-of-view designation with its appropriate full term by filling in the bubble with the corresponding number.

(26) cross-shot
(27) over-the-shoulder shot
(28) long shot

(29) extreme close-up
(30) medium shot
(31) extreme long shot

(32) close-up
(33) medium close-up
(34) two-shot

a. 2-S

b. LS

c. O/S

d. ELS

e. MCU

f. X/S

g. CU

h. ECU

i. MS

1a ○ ○ ○ ○ ○
26 27 28 29 30
○ ○ ○ ○
31 32 33 34

1b ○ ○ ○ ○ ○
26 27 28 29 30
○ ○ ○ ○
31 32 33 34

1c ○ ○ ○ ○ ○
26 27 28 29 30
○ ○ ○ ○
31 32 33 34

1d ○ ○ ○ ○ ○
26 27 28 29 30
○ ○ ○ ○
31 32 33 34

1e ○ ○ ○ ○ ○
26 27 28 29 30
○ ○ ○ ○
31 32 33 34

1f ○ ○ ○ ○ ○
26 27 28 29 30
○ ○ ○ ○
31 32 33 34

1g ○ ○ ○ ○ ○
26 27 28 29 30
○ ○ ○ ○
31 32 33 34

1h ○ ○ ○ ○ ○
26 27 28 29 30
○ ○ ○ ○
31 32 33 34

1i ○ ○ ○ ○ ○
26 27 28 29 30
○ ○ ○ ○
31 32 33 34

P A G E
T O T A L

© 2012 Wadsworth, Cengage Learning

Select the correct answers and fill in the bubbles with the corresponding numbers.

2. The shot sheet for (35) *camera 1* (36) *camera 2* is incorrect because it has
(37) *consecutive shot numbers* (38) *discontinuous shot numbers* (39) *an unworkable shot sequence* (40) *insufficient information for the director.* (**Multiple answers are possible.**)

2	◯ 35		◯ 36	
	◯ 37	◯ 38	◯ 39	◯ 40

C1

Shot #
1 CU of Kim
2 Follow her
3 Zoom To ECU
4 Truck left
5 Zoom in To CU of Kim
6 Dolly out

C2

Shot #
9 CU of Gary
12 O/S Gary/Kim
16 Follow Kim
20 MS door; pick up Kim leaving
21 Follow Frank coming in

PAGE TOTAL

© 2012 Wadsworth, Cengage Learning

3. Mark the following brief scene for a three-camera live-recorded studio production. Add any additional video cues you deem necessary. The scene takes place in the small office of a busy advertising executive. Draw a floor plan and prepare a shot sheet.

                    KIM
           (Bursts into Gary's office)

Let's go for coffee.

                    GARY

I don't have time.

                    KIM

Oh, shucks, make time.

                    GARY

You seem to be in a good mood today.

                    KIM

I'm always in a good mood...

                    GARY

Especially when I'm around.

                    KIM

I'm not so sure about that...but, yes, let's go.

                    GARY

I really don't...

                    KIM
(Walks behind Gary's desk and starts kissing his neck.)
Don't what?

                    GARY

Forget it. Let's go.

(The telephone rings. Gary turns to answer it, but then lets it
ring. He puts his arm around her. They both leave the office.)

© 2012 Wadsworth, Cengage Learning

4. Mark the following show opening of a series on basic video production. Memorize the cues so that you can devote your attention primarily to the preview monitors rather than to the script.

```
VIDEO BASICS SERIES
SHOW NO. 7
RECORDING DATE: July 15
AIR DATE: August 15

VIDEO                      AUDIO

Opening Server 2           Music SOS (sound on source)
:08 sec

CU of Phil                 PHIL
                           Hi, I'm Phil Kipper. Welcome to the
                           Broadcast and Electronic Communication
                           Arts Series, "Video Basics." As
                           promised last week, we will take you to a
                           special room where magic takes place:
                           the editing suite.

Pull out to reveal         PHIL
editing suite. Phil        Let me introduce to you the magician in
introduces Hamid.          charge, Hamid Khani, whose official title
CU of Hamid.               is senior postproduction editor.

2-shot                     (SAYS HELLO TO HAMID AND HAS
                           HAMID SAY HELLO TO THE AUDIENCE)
```

© 2012 Wadsworth, Cengage Learning

Select the correct answers and fill in the bubbles with the corresponding numbers.

5. The script markings in the following figure are (41) *acceptable* (42) *unacceptable* because they (43) *are too small* (44) *have unnecessary or redundant cues* (45) *are in the wrong place* (46) *show large, essential cues.* **(Fill in two bubbles.)**

5

41	42
○	○

43	44	45	46
○	○	○	○

JOHN

What's the matter?   *Ready camera 1*
                                      Ready to cue Tammy

TAMMY

Nothing.   *Cue Tammy and*
                                      take camera 1

JOHN

What do you mean, "nothing"? I can feel something is wrong.

TAMMY   *Ready to cue John*
                                      Ready to take camera 2

Well, I am glad you have some feeling left.

JOHN   *Cue John and take*
              camera 2

What's that supposed to mean?

TAMMY

Please, let's not start that again.

JOHN

Start what again?

TAMMY   *Ready to take camera 3*
                                      for a two-shot

Well, I guess it's time to talk.   *Take camera 3*

JOHN

What do you think we have been doing all this time?

PAGE TOTAL [   ]

SECTION TOTAL [   ]

© 2012 Wadsworth, Cengage Learning

REVIEW OF INTERPRETING STORYBOARDS

1. Each of the following four storyboards shows one or several major problems. Fill in the bubbles whose numbers correspond with one or more of these major problems: (47) *poor continuity and disturbance of the mental map* (48) *wrong field-of-view designation* (49) *wrong above- or below-eye-level camera position.* **(Note: Storyboards may exhibit more than one problem.)**

Storyboard a

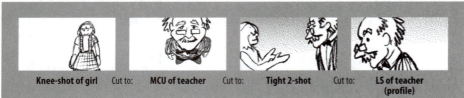

Knee-shot of girl Cut to: MCU of teacher Cut to: Tight 2-shot Cut to: LS of teacher (profile)

1a   ○ 47   ○ 48   ○ 49

Storyboard b

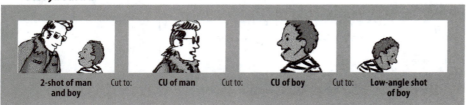

2-shot of man and boy Cut to: CU of man Cut to: CU of boy Cut to: Low-angle shot of boy

1b   ○ 47   ○ 48   ○ 49

Storyboard c

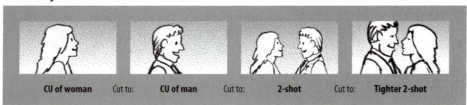

CU of woman Cut to: CU of man Cut to: 2-shot Cut to: Tighter 2-shot

1c   ○ 47   ○ 48   ○ 49

Storyboard d

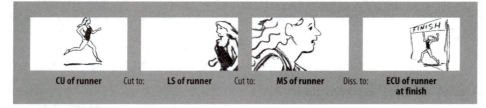

CU of runner Cut to: LS of runner Cut to: MS of runner Diss. to: ECU of runner at finish

1d   ○ 47   ○ 48   ○ 49

SECTION TOTAL [ ]

© 2012 Wadsworth, Cengage Learning

REVIEW OF SUPPORT STAFF

Identify the person mainly responsible for the following production activities and fill in the corresponding bubbles.

1. In elaborate multicamera productions or digital cinema, some of the scenes are sometimes directed by the (50) *floor manager* (51) *AD* (52) *PA.*

2. To put up and dress the new lawyer's set is the responsibility of the (53) *floor manager* (54) *art director* (55) *PA.*

3. In the absence of a property manager, props are usually handled by the (56) *floor manager* (57) *AD* (58) *art director.*

4. The novice news anchor would like to have the basic cues demonstrated. The cues should be demonstrated on the studio floor by the (59) *PA* (60) *floor manager* (61) *director.*

5. As the director, you want somebody to write down all major and minor problems that show up during rehearsal. For this job you would most likely ask the (62) *floor manager* (63) *producer* (64) *PA.*

1	○ 50	○ 51	○ 52
2	○ 53	○ 54	○ 55
3	○ 56	○ 57	○ 58
4	○ 59	○ 60	○ 61
5	○ 62	○ 63	○ 64

SECTION TOTAL [ ]

© 2012 Wadsworth, Cengage Learning

REVIEW OF TIME LINE

Select the correct answers and fill in the bubbles with the corresponding numbers.

1. Each of these time-line listings is (65) *acceptable* (66) *unacceptable,* because (67) *the time allotted for this production activity is appropriate* (68) *it allots too much time for the specific production activity* (69) *it allots too little time for the specific production activity.* **(Fill in two bubbles.)**

    a. Time Line May 25: Live-recorded 20-minute interview with college president on a standard interview set. She brings a model of the new library building, which needs to be set up in an adjacent area.

(1)	8:15 a.m.	Crew call
(2)	8:30–9:00 a.m.	Tech meeting
(3)	9:00–11:00 a.m.	Setup and lighting
(4)	11:00–11:30 a.m.	Lunch
(5)	11:30–11:45 a.m.	Notes and reset
(6)	11:45 a.m.–12:00 p.m.	Briefing of president (Green Room)
(7)	12:00–12:30 p.m.	Run-through and camera rehearsal

1a (1) ○ ○ 65 66 ○ ○ ○ 67 68 69

1a (2) ○ ○ 65 66 ○ ○ ○ 67 68 69

1a (3) ○ ○ 65 66 ○ ○ ○ 67 68 69

1a (4) ○ ○ 65 66 ○ ○ ○ 67 68 69

1a (5) ○ ○ 65 66 ○ ○ ○ 67 68 69

1a (6) ○ ○ 65 66 ○ ○ ○ 67 68 69

1a (7) ○ ○ 65 66 ○ ○ ○ 67 68 69

P A G E   T O T A L

W-56

© 2012 Wadsworth, Cengage Learning

(8)	12:30–12:45 p.m.	Notes	**1a** (8) ○ ○ 65 66 ○ ○ ○ 67 68 69
(9)	12:45–1:00 p.m.	Reset	**1a** (9) ○ ○ 65 66 ○ ○ ○ 67 68 69
(10)	1:00–1:10 p.m.	Break	**1a** (10) ○ ○ 65 66 ○ ○ ○ 67 68 69
(11)	1:10–1:45 p.m.	Record	**1a** (11) ○ ○ 65 66 ○ ○ ○ 67 68 69
(12)	1:45–1:55 p.m.	Spill	**1a** (12) ○ ○ 65 66 ○ ○ ○ 67 68 69
(13)	1:55–2:10 p.m.	Strike	**1a** (13) ○ ○ 65 66 ○ ○ ○ 67 68 69

b. Time Line June 2: Multicamera shoot for postproduction of two songs by a local rock group.

(1)	6:00 a.m.	Crew call	**1b** (1) ○ ○ 65 66 ○ ○ ○ 67 68 69
(2)	6:15–6:35 a.m.	Tech meeting	**1b** (2) ○ ○ 65 66 ○ ○ ○ 67 68 69
(3)	6:35–7:00 a.m.	Setup and lighting	**1b** (3) ○ ○ 65 66 ○ ○ ○ 67 68 69

PAGE TOTAL [   ]

© 2012 Wadsworth, Cengage Learning

Each of these time-line listings is (65) *acceptable* (66) *unacceptable,* because (67) *the time allotted for this production activity is appropriate* (68) *it allots too much time for the specific production activity* (69) *it allots too little time for the specific production activity.* **(Fill in two bubbles.)**

(4)	7:00–9:30 a.m.	Production meeting	
(5)	9:30 a.m.–12:30 p.m.	First run-through with cameras	
(6)	12:30–2:30 p.m.	Lunch	
(7)	2:30–2:45 p.m.	Record first song	
(8)	2:45–3:30 p.m.	Notes and reset	
(9)	3:30–5:00 p.m.	Record second song	
(10)	5:00–6:00 p.m.	Strike	

1b (4) ○ ○
65 66
○ ○ ○
67 68 69

1b (5) ○ ○
65 66
○ ○ ○
67 68 69

1b (6) ○ ○
65 66
○ ○ ○
67 68 69

1b (7) ○ ○
65 66
○ ○ ○
67 68 69

1b (8) ○ ○
65 66
○ ○ ○
67 68 69

1b (9) ○ ○
65 66
○ ○ ○
67 68 69

1b (10) ○ ○
65 66
○ ○ ○
67 68 69

PAGE TOTAL

SECTION TOTAL

© 2012 Wadsworth, Cengage Learning

▮ REVIEW QUIZ

*Mark the following statements as true or false by filling in the bubbles in the **T** (for true) or **F** (for false) column.*

		T	F
1.	The time line is the responsibility of the PA.	**1** ○ 70	○ 71
2.	The drama script format requires the full dialogue of all actors but only a minimum of visualization cues.	**2** ○ 72	○ 73
3.	A good floor plan will greatly facilitate camera and talent blocking.	**3** ○ 74	○ 75
4.	Proper visualization is essential for correct sequencing.	**4** ○ 76	○ 77
5.	Experienced floor managers will cue on their own if they think the director has missed a cue.	**5** ○ 78	○ 79
6.	Script marking is important when directing from a dramatic script and when directing from a two-column A/V script.	**6** ○ 80	○ 81
7.	Dramas are always fully scripted.	**7** ○ 82	○ 83
8.	If the script marking simply indicates "(2)" for one shot and "(3)" for the next, it implies that no "Ready" cues need be given.	**8** ○ 84	○ 85
9.	In a complex multicamera show, the AD will normally give stand-by cues.	**9** ○ 86	○ 87
10.	A storyboard shows the key visualization points of an event.	**10** ○ 88	○ 89
11.	When preparing camera shot sheets, the shots for each camera are listed in the order they appear in the script.	**11** ○ 90	○ 91
12.	Although the process message is important to the director in the production phase, it is relatively unimportant in preproduction.	**12** ○ 92	○ 93
13.	A good storyboard helps the director visualize a shot and determine camera positions.	**13** ○ 94	○ 95
14.	In a properly scripted documentary, all audio information is on page-left and all video information is on page-right.	**14** ○ 96	○ 97
15.	Because the director is engaged in artistic activities, knowledge of technical production aspects is relatively unimportant.	**15** ○ 98	○ 99
16.	The locking-in point means that you conjure up a vivid visual or aural image while analyzing the script.	**16** ○ 100	○ 101

SECTION TOTAL ▯

© 2012 Wadsworth, Cengage Learning

PROBLEM-SOLVING APPLICATIONS

1. The director of a weekly live sports show (consisting of a host and a prominent guest) tells the producer that she does not need a detailed script but that a show format will do just fine. What is your reaction?

2. When asked to direct an on-location television adaptation of a hit stage play, you are advised that the director of the play will determine the number and the positions of the cameras because he, after all, knows the stage blocking better than you do. What is your reaction? What would you suggest?

3. The director of a live-recorded segment of a new situation comedy tells you, the producer, that she has great difficulty deciding on optimal camera positions and marking the script because the art director has not yet finished the floor plan. What is your reaction? What would you suggest?

4. While you, the director, are preparing an EFP of a documentary segment on the lumber industry, the producer tells you not to worry too much about shot continuity because he intends to put the show together in extensive postproduction editing. Do you agree with the producer? If so, why? If not, why not?

5. The novice director proudly shows you, the producer, his marked show format for a live-recorded studio interview. He wrote out in longhand all the ready and take cues as well as all the cues for special effects. His writing takes up more space than the information of the show format. What is your reaction? Why?

6. If you were to describe to the producer what "locking-in" means when reading a dramatic script, what would you tell him?

7. The director of a number of successful digital movies tells you that "hearing" a shot can sometimes help the visualization process more than trying to "see" it. What does he mean by that?

8. Mark two or three scenes of a dramatic script, first for a three-camera live-recorded studio production and then for a single-camera studio production. Note the differences.

9. Prepare time lines for two studio productions and two EFPs.

10. Observe the scene while riding on a bus or train, waiting in line at an airport, eating lunch in a cafeteria, or sitting in a classroom listening to a lecture. How would you re-create and intensify one or all of these scenes for a multicamera or single-camera production?

© 2012 Wadsworth, Cengage Learning

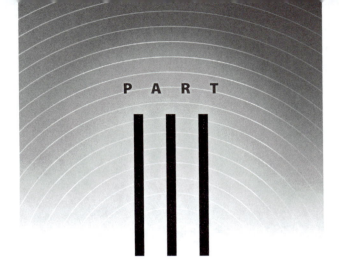

Production

© 2012 Wadsworth, Cengage Learning

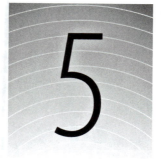

5 Analog and Digital Television

■ REVIEW OF KEY TERMS

Match each term with its appropriate definition by filling in the corresponding bubble.

1. refresh rate
2. sampling
3. interlaced scanning
4. 720p
5. compression
6. downloading

7. analog
8. frame
9. field
10. codec
11. HDTV

12. 1080i
13. RGB
14. progressive scanning
15. streaming
16. aspect ratio

A. A television standard with at least twice the picture detail of standard television

A	○ 1	○ 2	○ 3	○ 4
	○ 5	○ 6	○ 7	○ 8
	○ 9	○ 10	○ 11	○ 12
	○ 13	○ 14	○ 15	○ 16

B. Delivering and receiving digital video as continuous data

B	○ 1	○ 2	○ 3	○ 4
	○ 5	○ 6	○ 7	○ 8
	○ 9	○ 10	○ 11	○ 12
	○ 13	○ 14	○ 15	○ 16

PAGE
TOTAL

© 2012 Wadsworth, Cengage Learning

© 2012 Wadsworth, Cengage Learning

1. refresh rate	7. analog	12. 1080i	
2. sampling	8. frame	13. RGB	
3. interlaced scanning	9. field	14. progressive scanning	
4. 720p	10. codec	15. streaming	
5. compression	11. HDTV	16. aspect ratio	
6. downloading			

C. A system in which the electron beam starts scanning line 1, then line 2, then line 3, and so forth until all lines are scanned

C ○ ○ ○ ○
    1 2 3 4
    ○ ○ ○ ○
    5 6 7 8
    ○ ○ ○ ○
    9 10 11 12
    ○ ○ ○ ○
    13 14 15 16

D. The scanning of all odd-numbered scanning lines and the subsequent scanning of all even-numbered lines

D ○ ○ ○ ○
    1 2 3 4
    ○ ○ ○ ○
    5 6 7 8
    ○ ○ ○ ○
    9 10 11 12
    ○ ○ ○ ○
    13 14 15 16

E. The temporary rearrangement or elimination of redundant picture information for easier storage and signal transport

E ○ ○ ○ ○
    1 2 3 4
    ○ ○ ○ ○
    5 6 7 8
    ○ ○ ○ ○
    9 10 11 12
    ○ ○ ○ ○
    13 14 15 16

F. The transfer of files sent in data packets

F ○ ○ ○ ○
    1 2 3 4
    ○ ○ ○ ○
    5 6 7 8
    ○ ○ ○ ○
    9 10 11 12
    ○ ○ ○ ○
    13 14 15 16

P A G E
T O T A L

G. One-half of a complete scanning cycle

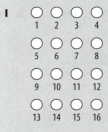

H. A complete interlaced scanning cycle

I. The basic colors of television

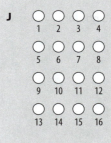

J. Progressive HDTV scanning system

K. A two-field interlaced scanning system for HDTV

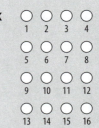

PAGE
TOTAL

© 2012 Wadsworth, Cengage Learning

1. refresh rate	7. analog	12. 1080i
2. sampling	8. frame	13. RGB
3. interlaced scanning	9. field	14. progressive scanning
4. 720p	10. codec	15. streaming
5. compression	11. HDTV	16. aspect ratio
6. downloading		

L. Selecting from an analog system a great many equally spaced signal values

L
1 2 3 4
5 6 7 8
9 10 11 12
13 14 15 16

M. The width-to-height proportion of a television screen

M
1 2 3 4
5 6 7 8
9 10 11 12
13 14 15 16

N. Stands for compressing and decompressing digital data

N
1 2 3 4
5 6 7 8
9 10 11 12
13 14 15 16

O. The number of complete frames per second

O
1 2 3 4
5 6 7 8
9 10 11 12
13 14 15 16

PAGE TOTAL

© 2012 Wadsworth, Cengage Learning

P.   Signal that fluctuates like the original stimulus

P
○ ○ ○ ○
1 2 3 4

○ ○ ○ ○
5 6 7 8

○ ○ ○ ○
9 10 11 12

○ ○ ○ ○
13 14 15 16

PAGE
TOTAL

SECTION
TOTAL

© 2012 Wadsworth, Cengage Learning

REVIEW OF ANALOG AND DIGITAL TELEVISION

Select the correct answers and fill in the bubbles with the corresponding numbers.

1. Digital television (17) *must use progressive scanning* (18) *must use interlaced scanning* (19) *can use either of the two systems.*

2. The four major steps of digitizing an analog signal are (20) *compression* (21) *analyzing* (22) *aliasing* (23) *anti-aliasing* (24) *quantizing* (25) *sampling* (26) *coding* (27) *digital-to-analog conversion* (28) *scanning.* ***(Fill in four bubbles.)***

3. The aspect ratio for wide-screen HDTV is (29) *4 × 3* (30) *16 × 9* (31) *16 × 4.*

4. The standard television (STV) format is (32) *4 × 3* (33) *9 × 3* (34) *16 × 9.*

5. Standard NTSC television uses a (35) *progressive* (36) *interlaced* (37) *compressed* scanning system.

6. One of the major advantages of digital television is that (38) *it always uses interlaced scanning* (39) *its picture does not deteriorate over numerous generations* (40) *it still uses analog signals.*

7. The two operational DTV systems are (41) *1080i* (42) *1280p* (43) *720p.* ***(Fill in two bubbles.)***

8. Which of the diagrams below represents most appropriately a digital signal?

(44)

(45)

(46)

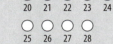

1	○ 17	○ 18	○ 19	
2	○ 20	○ 21	○ 22	○ 23 ○ 24
	○ 25	○ 26	○ 27	○ 28
3	○ 29	○ 30	○ 31	
4	○ 32	○ 33	○ 34	
5	○ 35	○ 36	○ 37	
6	○ 38	○ 39	○ 40	
7	○ 41	○ 42	○ 43	
8	○ 44	○ 45	○ 46	

SECTION TOTAL [   ]

© 2012 Wadsworth, Cengage Learning

REVIEW OF BASIC IMAGE CREATION AND THE COLORS OF THE VIDEO DISPLAY

Select the correct answers and fill in the bubbles with the corresponding numbers.

1. The basic television image is created by activating pixels that are (47) *arranged in a stack of vertical and horizontal lines* (48) *arranged in vertical columns only* (49) *randomly distributed.*

2. All the colors that you see on the television screen are a mixture of (50) *red, green, and blue* (51) *red, green, and yellow* (52) *red, blue, and yellow.*

3. The scanning can be (53) *only interlaced* (54) *only progressive* (55) *either interlaced or progressive.*

4. In progressive scanning, each scanning cycle produces (56) *a field* (57) *a frame* (58) *an interlaced field.*

5. The scanning of a complete NTSC frame takes (59) $\frac{1}{30}$ (60) $\frac{1}{60}$ (61) $\frac{1}{20}$ second.

6. HDTV can use (62) *interlaced or progressive scanning* (63) *only interlaced scanning* (64) *only progressive scanning.*

7. The 4K in digital cinema means that (65) *each horizontal line consists of 4,000 or more pixels* (66) *there are 4,000 potential colors* (67) *there are 4,000 frames per second.*

8. The refresh rate in progressive scanning (68) *is fixed at 30 fps* (69) *is fixed at 60 fps* (70) *can be variable.*

9. All other factors being equal, the highest-quality HDTV pictures are delivered by the (71) *480p system* (72) *720p system* (73) *1080i system.*

10. In progressive scanning (74) *only the even-numbered lines are scanned* (75) *only the odd-numbered lines are scanned* (76) *each line is scanned in a top-to-bottom sequence.*

Answer bubbles:

#			
1	47	48	49
2	50	51	52
3	53	54	55
4	56	57	58
5	59	60	61
6	62	63	64
7	65	66	67
8	68	69	70
9	71	72	73
10	74	75	76

SECTION TOTAL

© 2012 Wadsworth, Cengage Learning

REVIEW QUIZ

*Mark the following statements as true or false by filling in the bubbles in the **T** (for true) or **F** (for false) column.*

		T	F
1.	Analog recordings can tolerate more tape generations without noticeable loss than digital recordings.	○ 77	○ 78
2.	All flat-panel displays use LCD technology.	○ 79	○ 80
3.	RGB are the basic primary colors of analog as well as digital television.	○ 81	○ 82
4.	All digital video signals must be compressed before they can be recorded.	○ 83	○ 84
5.	The 16×9 aspect ratio is especially advantageous for showing an ECU of a face.	○ 85	○ 86
6.	Assigning 0's and 1's to the sampled signal is part of anti-aliasing.	○ 87	○ 88
7.	Digital signals are more robust but less complete than analog signals.	○ 89	○ 90
8.	A codec is a specific compression system.	○ 91	○ 92
9.	Downloading allows you to view continuous images and sound while the process is ongoing.	○ 93	○ 94
10.	In the digital process, sampling must precede quantizing.	○ 95	○ 96

SECTION TOTAL

© 2012 Wadsworth, Cengage Learning

PROBLEM-SOLVING APPLICATIONS

1. Your editor tells you that, contrary to sampling, which is an essential step in the digitization process, compression is not. Do you agree with the editor? If so, why? If not, why not?

2. The same editor insists on all-digital equipment with as high a sampling ratio and as little compression as possible because your projects require extensive postproduction with a great number of complex effects. What is your reaction? Why?

3. Your friend, an ardent movie fan, is extremely happy about the new 16 × 9 aspect ratio because, according to him, it is especially well suited to playing back old movies from the 1920s. Do you share his enthusiasm? If so, why? If not, why not?

4. Your organization intends to deliver video content via the Internet. Some members of the organization want the content streamed; others think that downloading is a better choice. List a few justifications for each argument.

5. The salesperson in a television store tells you that a digital television receiver can change the scanning standard, regardless of how the signals were originally sent. Is she correct? If not, why not?

6. You have been asked to select one of the HDTV systems (720p or 1080i) for your television studio. Describe each and justify why you would choose one over the other.

© 2012 Wadsworth, Cengage Learning

The Television Camera

REVIEW OF KEY TERMS

Match each term with its appropriate definition by filling in the corresponding bubble.

1. camera control unit
2. camera chain
3. HDTV camera
4. resolution
5. pixel

6. sync generator
7. white balance
8. imaging device
9. beam splitter
10. standard television

11. high-definition video
12. hue
13. saturation
14. brightness

A. The television system based on NTSC scanning

A
○ 1 ○ 2 ○ 3 ○ 4 ○ 5
○ 6 ○ 7 ○ 8 ○ 9 ○ 10
○ 11 ○ 12 ○ 13 ○ 14

B. How much light a color reflects; how dark or light a color appears on a black-and-white television screen

B
○ 1 ○ 2 ○ 3 ○ 4 ○ 5
○ 6 ○ 7 ○ 8 ○ 9 ○ 10
○ 11 ○ 12 ○ 13 ○ 14

C. Prism within a camera that separates white light into the three primary colors

C
○ 1 ○ 2 ○ 3 ○ 4 ○ 5
○ 6 ○ 7 ○ 8 ○ 9 ○ 10
○ 11 ○ 12 ○ 13 ○ 14

PAGE
TOTAL

© 2012 Wadsworth, Cengage Learning

1. camera control unit	6. sync generator	11. high-definition video
2. camera chain	7. white balance	12. hue
3. HDTV camera	8. imaging device	13. saturation
4. resolution	9. beam splitter	14. brightness
5. pixel	10. standard television	

D. The relative sharpness of the picture as measured by number of pixels

D
1 2 3 4 5
6 7 8 9 10
11 12 13 14

E. The camera connected with the CCU, power supply, and sync generator

E
1 2 3 4 5
6 7 8 9 10
11 12 13 14

F. The color itself (such as red or yellow)

F
1 2 3 4 5
6 7 8 9 10
11 12 13 14

G. Part of the camera chain; produces electronic synchronization signal

G
1 2 3 4 5
6 7 8 9 10
11 12 13 14

H. A unit, separate from the camera, that is used to process signals coming from and going to the camera to ensure optimal television pictures

H
1 2 3 4 5
6 7 8 9 10
11 12 13 14

PAGE TOTAL

© 2012 Wadsworth, Cengage Learning

I. Color strength or richness

I ○ ○ ○ ○ ○
   1 2 3 4 5
   ○ ○ ○ ○ ○
   6 7 8 9 10
   ○ ○ ○ ○
   11 12 13 14

J. Adjusting color circuits in a camera to produce a white color in lighting of various color temperatures

J ○ ○ ○ ○ ○
   1 2 3 4 5
   ○ ○ ○ ○ ○
   6 7 8 9 10
   ○ ○ ○ ○
   11 12 13 14

K. A video camera that delivers superior resolution, color, and contrast

K ○ ○ ○ ○ ○
   1 2 3 4 5
   ○ ○ ○ ○ ○
   6 7 8 9 10
   ○ ○ ○ ○
   11 12 13 14

L. The smallest single imaging element

L ○ ○ ○ ○ ○
   1 2 3 4 5
   ○ ○ ○ ○ ○
   6 7 8 9 10
   ○ ○ ○ ○
   11 12 13 14

M. The television system that produces high-resolution pictures that are highly compressed

M ○ ○ ○ ○ ○
   1 2 3 4 5
   ○ ○ ○ ○ ○
   6 7 8 9 10
   ○ ○ ○ ○
   11 12 13 14

N. The sensor mechanism in a camera that changes light into electrical energy

N ○ ○ ○ ○ ○
   1 2 3 4 5
   ○ ○ ○ ○ ○
   6 7 8 9 10
   ○ ○ ○ ○
   11 12 13 14

PAGE TOTAL _____

SECTION TOTAL _____

© 2012 Wadsworth, Cengage Learning

REVIEW OF BASIC CAMERA ELEMENTS AND FUNCTIONS

Select the correct answers and fill in the bubbles with the corresponding numbers.

1. The three basic parts of the camera are (15) *tally light* (16) *viewfinder* (17) *VR* (18) *imaging device, or sensor* (19) *lens* (20) *pedestal.* (**Fill in three bubbles.**)

   1   ○ 15   ○ 16   ○ 17
       ○ 18   ○ 19   ○ 20

2. Fill in the bubbles whose numbers correspond with the camera elements shown in the following figure.

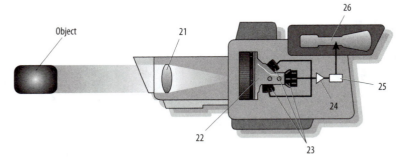

a. gathers and transmits the light

   2a ○ 21   ○ 22   ○ 23
       ○ 24   ○ 25   ○ 26

b. splits the white light into red, green, and blue light beams

   2b ○ 21   ○ 22   ○ 23
       ○ 24   ○ 25   ○ 26

c. processes video signal

   2c ○ 21   ○ 22   ○ 23
       ○ 24   ○ 25   ○ 26

d. converts signals back into visible screen images

   2d ○ 21   ○ 22   ○ 23
       ○ 24   ○ 25   ○ 26

e. amplifies video signals

   2e ○ 21   ○ 22   ○ 23
       ○ 24   ○ 25   ○ 26

f. transforms light into electric energy or video signals

   2f ○ 21   ○ 22   ○ 23
       ○ 24   ○ 25   ○ 26

PAGE
TOTAL

W-76

© 2012 Wadsworth, Cengage Learning

3. The camera imaging device is also called the (27) *ND filter* (28) *SD card* (29) *sensor.*

      3 ◯ 27   ◯ 28   ◯ 29

4. One of the following names describes a specific sensor: (30) *CCU* (31) *CMOS* (32) *chip.*

      4 ◯ 30   ◯ 31   ◯ 32

5. In some cameras the prism block is replaced by a (33) *CCD* (34) *lens* (35) *striped or mosaic filter array.*

      5 ◯ 33   ◯ 34   ◯ 35

6. The three basic parts of the camera chain are the (36) *power supply* (37) *prism block* (38) *lens* (39) *sync generator* (40) *camera head* (41) *viewfinder.* **(Fill in three bubbles.)**

      6 ◯ 36   ◯ 37   ◯ 38
          ◯ 39   ◯ 40   ◯ 41

7. To adjust a studio camera to produce optimal pictures, the VO must operate the (42) *CCU* (43) *CCD* (44) *HDV.*

      7 ◯ 42   ◯ 43   ◯ 44

8. An 8K digital cinema camera refers to (45) *a specific color temperature* (46) *the number of pixels on each horizontal scanning line* (47) *the number of vertical scanning lines.*

      8 ◯ 45   ◯ 46   ◯ 47

PAGE TOTAL ☐

SECTION TOTAL ☐

© 2012 Wadsworth, Cengage Learning

REVIEW OF ELECTRONIC OPERATIONAL FEATURES

Select the correct answers and fill in the bubbles with the corresponding numbers.

1. Most HD cameras let you switch between the aspect ratios of (48) *4 × 9 and 16 × 9* (49) *4 × 9 and 16 × 3* (50) *4 × 3 and 16 × 9.*

   1 ◯ 48   ◯ 49   ◯ 50

2. Most cameras allow you to switch between these audio standards: (51) *16 bit and 32 kHz* (52) *32 kHz and 48 kHz* (53) *16 bit and 48 kHz.*

   2 ◯ 51   ◯ 52   ◯ 53

3. Long-distance camera cables commonly used for transporting digital signals are (54) *IEEE 1394 and HDMI* (55) *FireWire and USB3* (56) *triax and fiber-optic.*

   3 ◯ 54   ◯ 55   ◯ 56

4. XLR connectors are used for (57) *digital video cables only* (58) *audio and video cables* (59) *audio cables only.*

   4 ◯ 57   ◯ 58   ◯ 59

5. A focus-assist feature is (60) *especially important for focusing small STV camcorders* (61) *especially important for focusing HDTV cameras* (62) *identical to auto-focus.*

   5 ◯ 60   ◯ 61   ◯ 62

SECTION TOTAL [   ]

© 2012 Wadsworth, Cengage Learning

REVIEW OF RESOLUTION, CONTRAST, AND COLOR

Select the correct answers and fill in the bubbles with the corresponding numbers.

1. Spatial resolution is determined by the number of (63) *scanning lines and pixels per line* (64) *frames per second* (65) *frame rate.*

2. Temporal resolution is determined by the (66) *number of frames per second* (67) *relative speed of a moving object* (68) *number of horizontal lines.*

3. In video "shading" means (69) *creating falloff electronically* (70) *adjusting the lighting for more shadows* (71) *controlling contrast.*

4. Contrast is a function of (72) *hue* (73) *saturation* (74) *brightness.*

5. The primary additive colors are (75) *LED* (76) *RGB* (77) *CMY.*

6. Television uses (78) *additive color mixing* (79) *color filter mixing* (80) *subtractive color mixing.*

7. The television color signal is processed as (81) *chrominance and color channels* (82) *luminance and chrominance* (83) *luminance and brightness.*

8. White-balancing adjusts the (84) *C channel* (85) *Y channel* (86) *z-axis.*

9. The C signal is responsible for the (87) *brightness* (88) *color* (89) *saturation* information.

10. The Y signal is responsible for the (90) *brightness* (91) *color* (92) *saturation* information.

1	○ 63	○ 64	○ 65
2	○ 66	○ 67	○ 68
3	○ 69	○ 70	○ 71
4	○ 72	○ 73	○ 74
5	○ 75	○ 76	○ 77
6	○ 78	○ 79	○ 80
7	○ 81	○ 82	○ 83
8	○ 84	○ 85	○ 86
9	○ 87	○ 88	○ 89
10	○ 90	○ 91	○ 92

SECTION TOTAL

© 2012 Wadsworth, Cengage Learning

REVIEW QUIZ

*Mark the following statements as true or false by filling in the bubbles in the **T** (for true) or **F** (for false) column.*

1. White-balancing adjusts the Y signals.

2. Digital data can be transferred by FireWire or with an HDMI cable.

3. An XLR plug is an audio connector.

4. Generally, studio cameras have higher-quality lenses than ENG camcorders.

5. A 720p scan always has a higher temporal resolution than a 480p scan.

6. You can use a neutral density filter to reduce the intensity of bright light.

7. RCA phono connectors can be used for digital video as well as audio signals.

8. A CMOS chip is similar in function to a CCD.

9. The camera sensor transduces (changes) electrical energy into light.

10. An S-video cable does not carry audio signals.

11. The sensor of a digital cinema camera normally is higher density than that of an HDTV camera.

	T	F
1	◯ 93	◯ 94
2	◯ 95	◯ 96
3	◯ 97	◯ 98
4	◯ 99	◯ 100
5	◯ 101	◯ 102
6	◯ 103	◯ 104
7	◯ 105	◯ 106
8	◯ 107	◯ 108
9	◯ 109	◯ 110
10	◯ 111	◯ 112
11	◯ 113	◯ 114

SECTION TOTAL

© 2012 Wadsworth, Cengage Learning

PROBLEM-SOLVING APPLICATIONS

1. List and describe four major features that distinguish a professional camcorder from a consumer camcorder.

2. When on an ENG assignment, you are forced to shoot in an extremely dark environment. There is no time to turn on any auxiliary lights, and your camcorder is not equipped with a camera light. What, if anything, can you do to produce visible images however noisy they may be?

3. When moving from indoor studio lighting to midday outdoor light, the field reporter tells you not to worry about white-balancing the camera again because the outside light of the foggy day seems to match the studio lighting anyway. What is your response? Why?

4. When watching a rehearsal of a dance company, the TD expresses concern because the dancers wear white leotards while performing a number in front of a black background. Is the TD's concern justified? If so, why? If not, why not? What are your recommendations?

5. The TD tells the camera operator that a high shutter speed needs a considerable amount of light. What does the TD mean by *shutter speed?* When do you need a high shutter speed? How, if at all, is it related to light levels?

6. Draw and describe the parts of the camera chain and their primary functions.

7. The TD assures the director that he can use a USB 3.0 SuperSpeed cable for connecting older equipment built for standard USB 2.0 cables. Is the TD's advice correct? If so, why? If not, why not?

7 Lenses

© 2012 Wadsworth, Cengage Learning

REVIEW OF KEY TERMS

Match each term with its appropriate definition by filling in the corresponding bubble.

1. **calibrate**
2. **depth of field**
3. **f-stop**
4. **wide-angle lens**

5. **fast lens**
6. **slow lens**
7. **zoom range**
8. **field of view**

9. **focal length**
10. **zoom lens**
11. **aperture**
12. **normal lens**

A. The distance from the optical center of the lens to the front surface of the camera imaging device

A ○ ○ ○ ○
   1 2 3 4
   ○ ○ ○ ○
   5 6 7 8
   ○ ○ ○ ○
   9 10 11 12

B. The area in which all objects, located at different distances from the camera, appear sharp and clear

B ○ ○ ○ ○
   1 2 3 4
   ○ ○ ○ ○
   5 6 7 8
   ○ ○ ○ ○
   9 10 11 12

C. Lens opening measured in *f*-stops

C ○ ○ ○ ○
   1 2 3 4
   ○ ○ ○ ○
   5 6 7 8
   ○ ○ ○ ○
   9 10 11 12

P A G E
T O T A L [   ]

1. calibrate	5. fast lens	9. focal length
2. depth of field	6. slow lens	10. zoom lens
3. *f*-stop	7. zoom range	11. aperture
4. wide-angle lens	8. field of view	12. normal lens

D. The general lens focal length that approximates the spatial relationships of normal vision

D ○ ○ ○ ○
　 1　2　3　4
　 ○ ○ ○ ○
　 5　6　7　8
　 ○ ○ ○ ○
　 9　10　11　12

E. Variable-focal-length lens, which can change from a wide shot to a close-up and vice versa in one continuous movement

E ○ ○ ○ ○
　 1　2　3　4
　 ○ ○ ○ ○
　 5　6　7　8
　 ○ ○ ○ ○
　 9　10　11　12

F. The extent of a scene that is visible through a particular lens

F ○ ○ ○ ○
　 1　2　3　4
　 ○ ○ ○ ○
　 5　6　7　8
　 ○ ○ ○ ○
　 9　10　11　12

G. To make a lens keep focus throughout the zoom

G ○ ○ ○ ○
　 1　2　3　4
　 ○ ○ ○ ○
　 5　6　7　8
　 ○ ○ ○ ○
　 9　10　11　12

H. A lens that at its maximum aperture permits a relatively small amount of light to enter and pass through

H ○ ○ ○ ○
　 1　2　3　4
　 ○ ○ ○ ○
　 5　6　7　8
　 ○ ○ ○ ○
　 9　10　11　12

P A G E
T O T A L　[　　　]

W-84

© 2012 Wadsworth, Cengage Learning

I. Same as short-focal-length lens, which gives a broad view of a scene

I ○ ○ ○ ○
1 2 3 4
○ ○ ○ ○
5 6 7 8
○ ○ ○ ○
9 10 11 12

J. The calibration on the lens indicating the diaphragm opening—and therefore the amount of light passing through the lens

J ○ ○ ○ ○
1 2 3 4
○ ○ ○ ○
5 6 7 8
○ ○ ○ ○
9 10 11 12

K. Shown in a focal-length ratio, such as 20:1

K ○ ○ ○ ○
1 2 3 4
○ ○ ○ ○
5 6 7 8
○ ○ ○ ○
9 10 11 12

L. A lens that at its maximum aperture permits a relatively great amount of light to enter and pass through

L ○ ○ ○ ○
1 2 3 4
○ ○ ○ ○
5 6 7 8
○ ○ ○ ○
9 10 11 12

PAGE
TOTAL

SECTION
TOTAL

© 2012 Wadsworth, Cengage Learning

▬ REVIEW OF OPTICAL CHARACTERISTICS OF LENSES

Select the correct answers and fill in the bubbles with the corresponding numbers.

1. Telephoto prime lenses, or zoom lenses in a narrow-angle position, have a relatively (13) *great* (14) *narrow* (15) *shallow* depth of field.

2. In a digital zoom, the focal length is adjusted by (16) *moving the camera closer to or farther away from the object* (17) *shifting certain lens elements* (18) *cropping the image while magnifying it.*

3. The focal length of zoom lenses that are built into small camcorders is generally (19) *not long enough when zoomed in* (20) *not short enough when zoomed out* (21) *fixed while zooming.*

4. Zoom lenses used for sports coverage need (22) *a lower zoom ratio than* (23) *a higher zoom ratio than* (24) *the same zoom ratio as* those used for studio work.

5. A wide-angle lens has a (25) *short* (26) *normal* (27) *long* focal length.

6. A 15x zoom lens means that you can increase the focal length (28) *1.5 times* (29) *150 times* (30) *15 times* in one continuous zoom.

7. When presetting (calibrating) the zoom lens, you (31) *zoom out all the way to a long shot, focus on the target object, and zoom back in again* (32) *zoom in all the way, focus on the target object, and zoom back.*

8. Large apertures (iris openings) contribute to a (33) *great* (34) *shallow* depth of field.

9. Select the three variables that influence depth of field: (35) *focal length of lens* (36) *zoom speed* (37) *focus* (38) *camera-to-object distance* (39) *lens aperture* (40) *focus mechanism.* **(Fill in three bubbles.)**

10. Given a fixed camera-to-object distance, short-focal-length lenses, or zoom lenses in the wide-angle position, have a relatively (41) *shallow* (42) *wide* (43) *great* depth of field.

11. The area in which all objects, although located at different distances from the camera, are in focus is called (44) *depth of focus* (45) *field of view* (46) *depth of field.*

12. In an optical zoom, the focal length is adjusted by (47) *shifting certain lens elements* (48) *shifting the pixels* (49) *moving the camera closer to or farther away from the object.*

#			
1	○ 13	○ 14	○ 15
2	○ 16	○ 17	○ 18
3	○ 19	○ 20	○ 21
4	○ 22	○ 23	○ 24
5	○ 25	○ 26	○ 27
6	○ 28	○ 29	○ 30
7	○ 31	○ 32	
8	○ 33	○ 34	
9	○ 35	○ 36	○ 37
	○ 38	○ 39	○ 40
10	○ 41	○ 42	○ 43
11	○ 44	○ 45	○ 46
12	○ 47	○ 48	○ 49

PAGE TOTAL [   ]

© 2012 Wadsworth, Cengage Learning

13. Assuming maximum aperture, a slow lens (50) *transmits an image faster* (51) *transmits an image more slowly* (52) *permits more light to enter* (53) *permits less light to enter* than does a fast lens.

13 ○ ○ ○ ○
   50 51 52 53

14. Assuming maximum aperture, a fast lens (54) *transmits an image faster* (55) *transmits an image more slowly* (56) *permits more light to enter* (57) *permits less light to enter* than does a slow lens.

14 ○ ○ ○ ○
   54 55 56 57

15. In the diagram below, select the most appropriate *f*-stop number for each of the four apertures (**a** through **d**) and fill in the bubbles with the corresponding number.

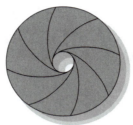

a. (58) *f*/ 5.6 (59) *f*/ 1.4 (60) *f*/22

15a ○   ○   ○
    58   59   60

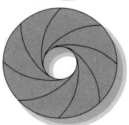

b. (61) *f*/16 (62) *f*/2.8 (63) *f*/1.4

15b ○   ○   ○
    61   62   63

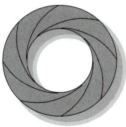

c. (64) *f*/1.4 (65) *f*/4 (66) *f*/16

15c ○   ○   ○
    64   65   66

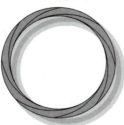

d. (67) *f*/ 22 (68) *f*/8 (69) *f*/1.4

15d ○   ○   ○
    67   68   69

PAGE TOTAL [   ]

SECTION TOTAL [   ]

© 2012 Wadsworth, Cengage Learning

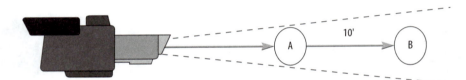

REVIEW OF HOW LENSES SEE

Select the correct answers and fill in the bubbles with the corresponding numbers.

1. A wide-angle lens (70) *increases* (71) *decreases* the illusion of depth and (72) *increases* (73) *decreases* the speed of an object moving toward or away from the camera. ***(Fill in two bubbles.)***

2. To apply selective focus, we need (74) *a great* (75) *a shallow* depth of field.

3. A narrow-angle lens makes objects positioned at different distances from the camera look (76) *more* (77) *less* crowded than they really are and (78) *increases* (79) *decreases* the speed of an object moving toward or away from the camera. ***(Fill in two bubbles.)***

4. To make a small room look larger, we use (80) *a wide-angle* (81) *a narrow-angle* lens.

5. The figure below shows the camera zoomed in all the way for a telephoto view and focused on object A. Object B will probably be (82) *in focus* (83) *out of focus*. The depth of field is therefore (84) *great* (85) *shallow*. ***(Fill in two bubbles.)***

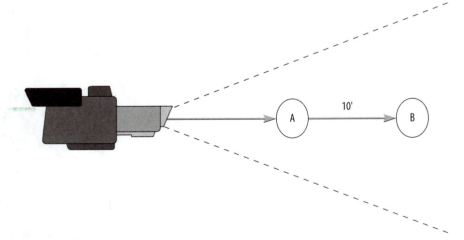

6. The figure below shows the camera zoomed out all the way for a wide-angle view and focused on object A. Object B will probably be (86) *in focus* (87) *out of focus*. The depth of field is therefore (88) *great* (89) *shallow*. ***(Fill in two bubbles.)***

1	○ 70	○ 71
	○ 72	○ 73
2	○ 74	○ 75
3	○ 76	○ 77
	○ 78	○ 79
4	○ 80	○ 81
5	○ 82	○ 83
	○ 84	○ 85
6	○ 86	○ 87
	○ 88	○ 89

P A G E
T O T A L

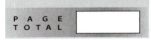

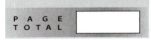

© 2012 Wadsworth, Cengage Learning

7. The screen image below displays a (90) *shallow* (91) *great* depth of field.

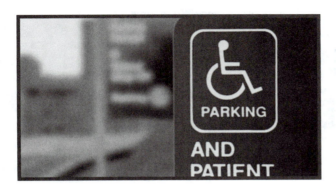

8. The screen image below shows that the camera's zoom lens was in a (92) *narrow-angle* position (93) *wide-angle*.

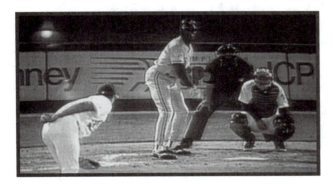

9. The opening shot of a documentary on city politics shows the city hall through a piece of sculpture. The camera operator used (94) *a wide-angle* (95) *a narrow-angle* position.

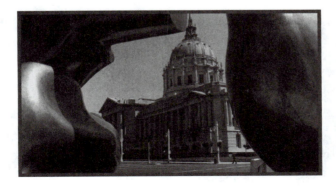

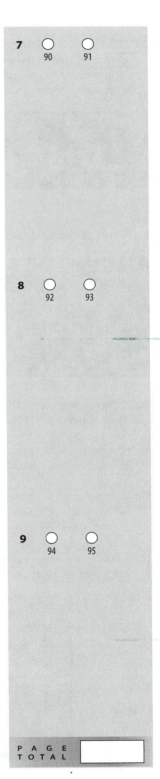

PHOTO: HERBERT ZETTL

PHOTO: HERBERT ZETTL

PHOTO: CHIRS ROZALES

© 2012 Wadsworth, Cengage Learning

10. Your preview monitors for cameras 1, 2, and 3 display the following images. Assuming that all three cameras are positioned right next to one another, which is the approximate zoom position for each? Choose among (96) *wide angle* (97) *normal* and (98) *narrow angle.*

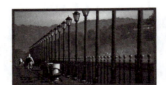
Camera 1

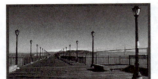
Camera 2

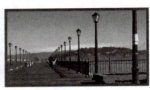
Camera 3

11. The figure below simulates (99) *a digital zoom* (100) *an optical zoom.*

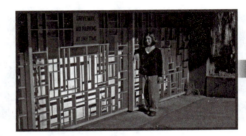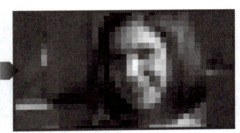

12. When zoomed in on somebody approaching the camera, the person seems to move (101) *slower than* (102) *about the same speed as* (103) *faster than* they actually do.

13. The closer the camera is to the object, the (104) *shallower* (105) *greater* (106) *wider* the depth of field becomes.

14. Assuming that your image stabilizer is disengaged, you can avoid handheld camera wobbles by (107) *zooming all the way in* (108) *zooming all the way out* (109) *keeping the zoom lens in the narrow-angle position.*

15. In the screen image below, the zoom lens was in the (110) *normal* (111) *narrow-angle* (112) *wide-angle* zoom position.

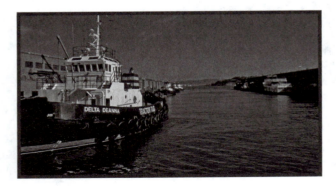

10	C1	○ 96	○ 97	○ 98
	C2	○ 96	○ 97	○ 98
	C3	○ 96	○ 97	○ 98

11	○ 99	○ 100

12	○ 101	○ 102	○ 103

13	○ 104	○ 105	○ 106

14	○ 107	○ 108	○ 109

15	○ 110	○ 111	○ 112

PAGE TOTAL

SECTION TOTAL

PHOTOS: HERBERT ZETTL

PHOTOS: HERBERT ZETTL

PHOTO: HERBERT ZETTL

© 2012 Wadsworth, Cengage Learning

REVIEW QUIZ

*Mark the following statements as true or false by filling in the bubbles in the **T** (for true) or **F** (for false) column.*

		T	F
1.	Auto-focus and focus-assist features are the same.	○ 113	○ 114
2.	A zoom can be simulated by gradually enlarging the image's center portion.	○ 115	○ 116
3.	Depth of field is influenced only by the focal length of the lens.	○ 117	○ 118
4.	Depth of field increases as focal length decreases.	○ 119	○ 120
5.	When covering a news story with an ENG/EFP camera, you are best off with a shallow depth of field because there are few, if any, focusing problems.	○ 121	○ 122
6.	A slow lens is one with a very low f-stop number, such as $f/1.4$.	○ 123	○ 124
7.	After the initial calibration of a zoom lens, you need to preset it again each time the distance from object to camera changes substantially.	○ 125	○ 126
8.	When calibrating a zoom lens, you must first zoom in on the target object and focus and then zoom out.	○ 127	○ 128
9.	An object moving toward the camera looks faster than normal when shot with a wide-angle lens.	○ 129	○ 130
10.	Because a 1080i HDTV image has so many scanning lines, the lens quality is relatively unimportant.	○ 131	○ 132
11.	Digital and optical zooms work on the same principle.	○ 133	○ 134
12.	Each time you stop a zoom from one extreme position to the next, you get a different focal length.	○ 135	○ 136
13.	Compared with an optical zoom, a digital zoom permits a higher zoom ratio without picture deterioration.	○ 137	○ 138
14.	We can dolly most easily when the lens is in the extreme wide-angle position.	○ 139	○ 140
15.	Digital stabilizers can absorb all picture wobble when you are shooting a narrow-angle picture.	○ 141	○ 142
16.	One of the major differences between a studio HDTV camera and a digital cinema camera is that the latter has a much higher-density sensor.	○ 143	○ 144

SECTION TOTAL [   ]

© 2012 Wadsworth, Cengage Learning

PROBLEM-SOLVING APPLICATIONS

Let us now put the theory to work. You can observe the optical and performance characteristics of lenses easily by using a camcorder or a still camera that can accept various lenses. Think through each production problem and consider the various options; then pick the most effective solution and justify your choice.

1. Zoom all the way out with the camcorder, or attach a wide-angle lens (28mm or less focal length) to the single-lens reflex (SLR) still camera, and focus on an object 4 to 6 feet away from you. Look at the background objects (20 or so feet away from you). Are they visible? Do they appear in fairly sharp focus? Or are they blurred? Now do the same observations by zooming all the way in or by attaching a telephoto lens (with a focal length of 200mm) to the still camera. Explain depth-of-field characteristics.

2. When watching television or a movie, try to figure out what lenses were used for some of the shots. For example, when you see someone running toward the camera yet seemingly not getting closer, what lens was used? Or when you see the happy couple approach the dinner table through the flowers and the candles in the foreground, what lens was probably used, assuming that the couple, as well as the candles and the flowers, are in focus? Such observations will certainly help you become more aware of focal lengths and their effects.

3. You are the AD of a live telecast of a modern dance program, which is performed on a dimly lighted stage. The operators of the two key cameras express some concern about their lenses. The new lens of the handheld ENG/EFP camera 1 has a 25× zoom range and a maximum aperture of ƒ/5.6. Although the lens was used successfully during the past three football games, the operator feels that it might be too slow for this type of application. Camera 2 has a 10× lens with a 2× range extender. Its maximum aperture is also ƒ/5.6. Are the operators' concerns justified?

4. The novice director asks you, the operator of camera 3, to get the opening shot by zooming back slowly from an extreme close-up of the title of a book to an extreme wide shot that shows a large part of the studio (the other cameras, the floor manager, the overhead lighting) as the background for the opening titles. The director sets up the wide shot first to make sure that it shows enough of the studio. When your extreme-narrow-angle zoom lens position does not produce the desired close-up of the book title, he asks you to "simply pop in a range extender before we punch up your camera." What are the potential problems, if any? Be specific.

5. While shooting a dramatic program in the studio, you, the camera 1 operator, are told by the director that your camera shows the scratched background walls in sharp focus. The director asks you to make the walls look slightly out of focus without impeding the sharp focus on the foreground talent. What would you do?

© 2012 Wadsworth, Cengage Learning

Camera Operation and Picture Composition

REVIEW OF KEY TERMS

Match each term with its appropriate definition by filling in the corresponding bubble.

1. close-up
2. closure
3. cross-shot
4. field of view
5. headroom
6. noseroom
7. leadroom

8. over-the-shoulder shot
9. z-axis
10. monopod
11. arc
12. dolly
13. cant
14. truck

15. camera stabilizing system
16. robotic pedestal
17. tilt
18. quick-release plate
19. pan
20. studio pan-and-tilt head

A. Object or any part of it seen at close range

B. To move the camera laterally by means of a mobile camera mount

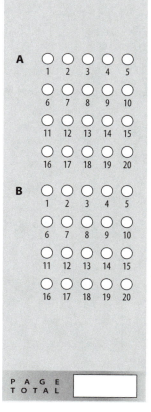

© 2012 Wadsworth, Cengage Learning

1. close-up	8. over-the-shoulder shot	15. camera stabilizing system
2. closure	9. z-axis	16. robotic pedestal
3. cross-shot	10. monopod	17. tilt
4. field of view	11. arc	18. quick-release plate
5. headroom	12. dolly	19. pan
6. noseroom	13. cant	20. studio pan-and-tilt head
7. leadroom	14. truck	

C. The space left between the top of the head and the upper screen edge

D. Camera looks at the camera-far person with the back and shoulder of the camera-near person in the shot

E. The space left in front of an object or a person moving toward the edge of the screen

F. A single pole onto which you can mount a camera

PAGE TOTAL

© 2012 Wadsworth, Cengage Learning

G. To point the camera up or down

H. To move the camera in a slightly curved dolly or truck

I. To tilt a handheld camera sideways

J. Similar to the over-the-shoulder shot except that the camera-near person is completely out of the shot

K. Portion of a scene visible through a particular lens; its vista

G 1 2 3 4 5 / 6 7 8 9 10 / 11 12 13 14 15 / 16 17 18 19 20

H 1 2 3 4 5 / 6 7 8 9 10 / 11 12 13 14 15 / 16 17 18 19 20

I 1 2 3 4 5 / 6 7 8 9 10 / 11 12 13 14 15 / 16 17 18 19 20

J 1 2 3 4 5 / 6 7 8 9 10 / 11 12 13 14 15 / 16 17 18 19 20

K 1 2 3 4 5 / 6 7 8 9 10 / 11 12 13 14 15 / 16 17 18 19 20

PAGE TOTAL ☐

© 2012 Wadsworth, Cengage Learning

1. close-up	8. over-the-shoulder shot	15. camera stabilizing system
2. closure	9. z-axis	16. robotic pedestal
3. cross-shot	10. monopod	17. tilt
4. field of view	11. arc	18. quick-release plate
5. headroom	12. dolly	19. pan
6. noseroom	13. cant	20. studio pan-and-tilt head
7. leadroom	14. truck	

L. Imaginary line extending from the lens to the horizon

M. Device to attach an ENG/EFP camera to the mounting head

N. Mentally filling in spaces of an incomplete picture

O. The space left in front of a person looking toward the screen edge

L
○1 ○2 ○3 ○4 ○5
○6 ○7 ○8 ○9 ○10
○11 ○12 ○13 ○14 ○15
○16 ○17 ○18 ○19 ○20

M
○1 ○2 ○3 ○4 ○5
○6 ○7 ○8 ○9 ○10
○11 ○12 ○13 ○14 ○15
○16 ○17 ○18 ○19 ○20

N
○1 ○2 ○3 ○4 ○5
○6 ○7 ○8 ○9 ○10
○11 ○12 ○13 ○14 ○15
○16 ○17 ○18 ○19 ○20

O
○1 ○2 ○3 ○4 ○5
○6 ○7 ○8 ○9 ○10
○11 ○12 ○13 ○14 ○15
○16 ○17 ○18 ○19 ○20

PAGE
TOTAL

© 2012 Wadsworth, Cengage Learning

P. To move the camera toward or away from an object

P
- ( )1 ( )2 ( )3 ( )4 ( )5
- ( )6 ( )7 ( )8 ( )9 ( )10
- ( )11 ( )12 ( )13 ( )14 ( )15
- ( )16 ( )17 ( )18 ( )19 ( )20

Q. Horizontal turning of the camera

Q
- ( )1 ( )2 ( )3 ( )4 ( )5
- ( )6 ( )7 ( )8 ( )9 ( )10
- ( )11 ( )12 ( )13 ( )14 ( )15
- ( )16 ( )17 ( )18 ( )19 ( )20

R. Mounting head for heavy cameras that permits extremely smooth movements

R
- ( )1 ( )2 ( )3 ( )4 ( )5
- ( )6 ( )7 ( )8 ( )9 ( )10
- ( )11 ( )12 ( )13 ( )14 ( )15
- ( )16 ( )17 ( )18 ( )19 ( )20

S. Computer-controlled camera mount

S
- ( )1 ( )2 ( )3 ( )4 ( )5
- ( )6 ( )7 ( )8 ( )9 ( )10
- ( )11 ( )12 ( )13 ( )14 ( )15
- ( )16 ( )17 ( )18 ( )19 ( )20

T. Camera mount that helps produce jitter-free pictures even when the camera operator runs with it

T
- ( )1 ( )2 ( )3 ( )4 ( )5
- ( )6 ( )7 ( )8 ( )9 ( )10
- ( )11 ( )12 ( )13 ( )14 ( )15
- ( )16 ( )17 ( )18 ( )19 ( )20

PAGE TOTAL [ ]

SECTION TOTAL [ ]

© 2012 Wadsworth, Cengage Learning

■ **REVIEW OF CAMERA MOVEMENTS
AND CAMERA SUPPORTS**

Select the correct answers and fill in the bubbles with the corresponding numbers.

1. Fill in the bubbles whose numbers correspond with the camera movements indicated in the following figure.

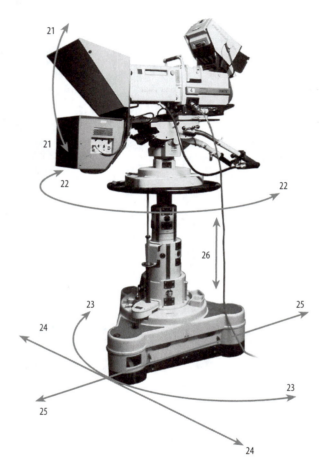

a. pedestal

b. truck

c. pan

d. tilt

e. dolly

f. arc

<table>
<tr><td>**1a**</td><td>○ 21</td><td>○ 22</td><td>○ 23</td></tr>
<tr><td></td><td>○ 24</td><td>○ 25</td><td>○ 26</td></tr>
<tr><td>**1b**</td><td>○ 21</td><td>○ 22</td><td>○ 23</td></tr>
<tr><td></td><td>○ 24</td><td>○ 25</td><td>○ 26</td></tr>
<tr><td>**1c**</td><td>○ 21</td><td>○ 22</td><td>○ 23</td></tr>
<tr><td></td><td>○ 24</td><td>○ 25</td><td>○ 26</td></tr>
<tr><td>**1d**</td><td>○ 21</td><td>○ 22</td><td>○ 23</td></tr>
<tr><td></td><td>○ 24</td><td>○ 25</td><td>○ 26</td></tr>
<tr><td>**1e**</td><td>○ 21</td><td>○ 22</td><td>○ 23</td></tr>
<tr><td></td><td>○ 24</td><td>○ 25</td><td>○ 26</td></tr>
<tr><td>**1f**</td><td>○ 21</td><td>○ 22</td><td>○ 23</td></tr>
<tr><td></td><td>○ 24</td><td>○ 25</td><td>○ 26</td></tr>
</table>

PAGE
TOTAL

PHOTO: EDWARD AIONA

© 2012 Wadsworth, Cengage Learning

2. The spreader (27) *keeps the tripod legs from spreading too far* (28) *must always be fully extended* (29) *helps spread the tripod legs as much as possible.*

2	○ 27	○ 28	○ 29

3. The (30) *leveling bowl* (31) *monopod* (32) *jib arm* helps maintain a camera in a horizontal position.

3	○ 30	○ 31	○ 32

4. Mounting heads facilitate (33) *dollies and trucks* (34) *smooth tilts and pans* (35) *arcs and zooms.*

4	○ 33	○ 34	○ 35

5. A (36) *wedge mount* (37) *robotic pedestal* (38) *quick-release plate* makes it easy to detach an ENG/EFP camera from the tripod and reattach it again.

5	○ 36	○ 37	○ 38

6. Compared with a tripod, a studio pedestal allows these additional camera moves: (39) *canting left and right* (40) *raising and lowering the camera while on the air* (41) *booming up and down.*

6	○ 39	○ 40	○ 41

7. To simultaneously boom, tongue, pan, and tilt the camera, you need a (42) *robotic pedestal* (43) *jib arm* (44) *camera stabilizing system.*

7	○ 42	○ 43	○ 44

8. The camera support that allows the camera operator to run with the camera while keeping the picture steady is a (45) *robotic arm* (46) *Steadicam* (47) *jib arm.*

8	○ 45	○ 46	○ 47

9. The camera support that allows the operator of a small handheld camera to walk or run without any picture wobbles is a (48) *Steadicam* (49) *monopod* (50) *handheld stabilizer.*

9	○ 48	○ 49	○ 50

PAGE TOTAL [ ]

SECTION TOTAL [ ]

© 2012 Wadsworth, Cengage Learning

REVIEW OF HOW TO WORK A CAMERA

Select the correct answers and fill in the bubbles with the corresponding numbers.

1. When dollying with a studio camera or walking with an EFP camera, the depth of field should be as (51) *shallow* (52) *great* (53) *narrow* as possible.

1	○ 51	○ 52	○ 53

2. To minimize camera wobbles when dollying with a studio camera or walking with an EFP camera, the zoom lens should be in a (54) *narrow-angle* (55) *wide-angle* (56) *telephoto* position.

2	○ 54	○ 55	○ 56

3. After having calibrated the zoom lens, you need to preset it again (57) *only when the camera moves* (58) *only when the object moves relative to the camera* (59) *whenever camera or object moves relative to the other.*

3	○ 57	○ 58	○ 59

4. When operating a camcorder in the field, you should always have the camera mic (60) *on* (61) *off* (62) *replaced by a shotgun mic.*

4	○ 60	○ 61	○ 62

5. When panning with a shoulder-mounted ENG/EFP camera, you should point your knees toward (63) *the starting point of the pan* (64) *the end point of the pan* (65) *either direction.*

5	○ 63	○ 64	○ 65

6. During a test recording with your ENG/EFP camcorder, you should (66) *leave the lens cap on but check the audio* (67) *make sure all camera features are working* (68) *ask the reporter to count to 10.*

6	○ 66	○ 67	○ 68

7. When loading a VTR cassette or memory card for recording, the safety tab (69) *does not matter because it is primarily meant for playback protection* (70) *should be in the open position* (71) *should be in place or in the closed position.*

7	○ 69	○ 70	○ 71

8. When on an ENG assignment, you should record ambient sound (72) *only if somebody is talking* (73) *only if there is no background noise* (74) *always.*

8	○ 72	○ 73	○ 74

9. To calibrate a zoom lens (75) *zoom in, focus, zoom out* (76) *zoom out, focus, zoom in* (77) *adjust focus continuously while zooming.*

9	○ 75	○ 76	○ 77

10. When calibrating a zoom lens, the tally light should be (78) *on* (79) *off* (80) *ignored.*

10	○ 78	○ 79	○ 80

11. To achieve critical focus when operating an HDTV studio camera, you should (81) *adjust the viewfinder's sharpness* (82) *engage the auto-focus feature* (83) *engage the focus-assist feature.*

11	○ 81	○ 82	○ 83

12. You should lock the camera mounting head (84) *every time you leave it* (85) *only when temporarily leaving the camera* (86) *at the end of the shoot.*

12	○ 84	○ 85	○ 86

PAGE TOTAL _____

© 2012 Wadsworth, Cengage Learning

13. When leaving a studio camera temporarily unattended, you should (87) *tighten the lock mechanism* (88) *tighten the drag control* (89) *point the camera toward the floor rather than into the lights.*

13 ○ ○ ○
    87 88 89

14. When trying to preserve battery power, you should switch off (90) *only the foldout monitor* (91) *only the image stabilizer* (92) *both the foldout monitor and the image stabilizer.*

14 ○ ○ ○
    90 91 92

15. When operating the camcorder in EFP, you should engage the audio AGC (93) *always* (94) *never* (95) *only when necessary.*

15 ○ ○ ○
    93 94 95

16. When operating a studio camera, the electronic adjustments for optimal picture quality are made for you by the (96) *VO* (97) *TD* (98) *AD.*

16 ○ ○ ○
    96 97 98

PAGE TOTAL [ ]

SECTION TOTAL [ ]

© 2012 Wadsworth, Cengage Learning

REVIEW OF FRAMING EFFECTIVE SHOTS

1. Using the set of numbered images below, fill in the bubbles for each of the following fields of view or shot designations.

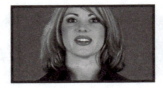

99

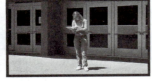

100

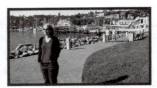

101

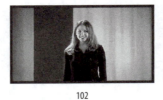

102

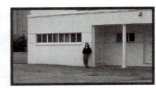

103

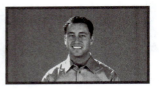

104

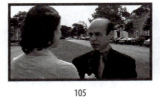

105

106

107

a. ELS (extreme long shot)

1a ◯ ◯ ◯ ◯ ◯
99 100 101 102 103

◯ ◯ ◯ ◯
104 105 106 107

b. LS (long shot)

1b ◯ ◯ ◯ ◯ ◯
99 100 101 102 103

◯ ◯ ◯ ◯
104 105 106 107

PAGE
TOTAL

PHOTOS: EDWARD AIONA

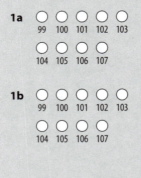

© 2012 Wadsworth, Cengage Learning

c. MS (medium shot)

1c	99	100	101	102	103
	104	105	106	107	

d. bust shot

1d	99	100	101	102	103
	104	105	106	107	

e. knee shot

1e	99	100	101	102	103
	104	105	106	107	

f. three-shot

1f	99	100	101	102	103
	104	105	106	107	

g. ECU (extreme close-up)

1g	99	100	101	102	103
	104	105	106	107	

h. CU (close-up)

1h	99	100	101	102	103
	104	105	106	107	

i. over-the-shoulder shot

1i	99	100	101	102	103
	104	105	106	107	

PAGE TOTAL [   ]

© 2012 Wadsworth, Cengage Learning

2. Evaluate the framing of shots in the next five figures by filling in the bubbles with the corresponding numbers. *(Note: There may be more than one correct answer for some parts of a problem.)*

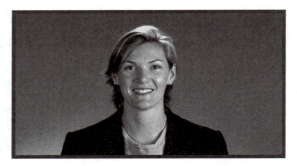

a. This CU is (108) *acceptable* (109) *unacceptable* because it has (110) *no headroom* (111) *too much headroom* (112) *adequate headroom* (113) *adequate noseroom*. If unacceptable, you should (114) *tilt up* (115) *tilt down* (116) *pan left*.

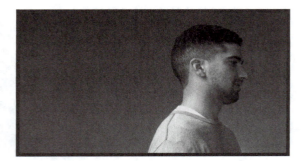

b. This shot is (117) *acceptable* (118) *unacceptable* because it has (119) *sufficient noseroom* (120) *insufficient noseroom* (121) *sufficient headroom* (122) *insufficient leadroom*. If unacceptable, you should (123) *pan left* (124) *pan right* (125) *tilt up* (126) *tilt down* (127) *pedestal up* (128) *pedestal down*.

2a
○ 108   ○ 109
○ 110 ○ 111 ○ 112 ○ 113
○ 114 ○ 115 ○ 116

2b
○ 117   ○ 118
○ 119 ○ 120 ○ 121 ○ 122
○ 123 ○ 124 ○ 125
○ 126 ○ 127 ○ 128

PAGE TOTAL ☐

PHOTO: EDWARD AIONA

PHOTO: EDWARD AIONA

© 2012 Wadsworth, Cengage Learning

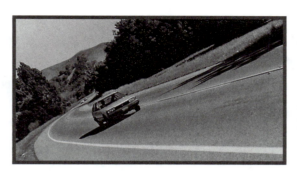

c. This shot is intended to emphasize the car's speed and risky driving. Its framing is therefore (129) *acceptable* (130) *unacceptable*. If unacceptable, you should (131) *level the horizon line* (132) *zoom out*.

2c ○ 129   ○ 130
    ○ 131   ○ 132

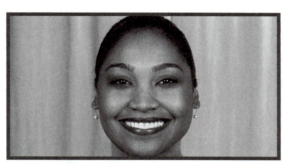

d. This shot is (133) *acceptable* (134) *unacceptable* because it has (135) *no headroom* (136) *too much headroom* (137) *no noseroom* (138) *no leadroom* (139) *insufficient clues for closure in off-screen space*. If unacceptable, you should (140) *tilt up* (141) *tilt down*.

2d ○ 133   ○ 134
    ○ 135 ○ 136 ○ 137 ○ 138 ○ 139
    ○ 140   ○ 141

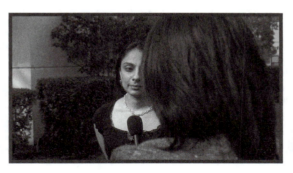

e. This over-the-shoulder shot is (142) *acceptable* (143) *unacceptable*. If unacceptable, you should (144) *zoom out* (145) *pedestal up* (146) *arc left* (147) *arc right*.

2e ○ 142   ○ 143
    ○ 144 ○ 145 ○ 146 ○ 147

PAGE TOTAL [   ]

PHOTO: HERBERT ZETTL

PHOTO: EDWARD AIONA

PHOTO: EDWARD AIONA

© 2012 Wadsworth, Cengage Learning

3. This shot makes (148) *good* (149) *poor* use of screen depth because (150) *it lacks foreground objects* (151) *the horizon is too high.*

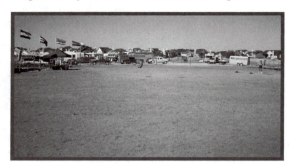

4. This framing is (152) *acceptable* (153) *unacceptable* in terms of closure.

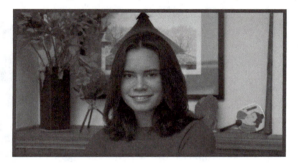

PHOTO: HERBERT ZETTL

PHOTO: EDWARD AIONA

3
○ 148   ○ 149
○ 150   ○ 151

4
○ 152   ○ 153

P A G E
T O T A L

S E C T I O N
T O T A L

© 2012 Wadsworth, Cengage Learning

REVIEW QUIZ

*Mark the following statements as true or false by filling in the bubbles in the **T** (for true) or **F** (for false) column.*

		T	F
1.	Once balanced, the wedge mount ensures that the camera is mounted in an optimally balanced position for each subsequent use.	**1** ○ 154	○ 155
2.	Psychological closure always ensures good composition.	**2** ○ 156	○ 157
3.	The studio pedestal permits very-low-angle shots.	**3** ○ 158	○ 159
4.	You should unlock the pan-and-tilt mechanism at the beginning of the show and lock it again every time you leave the camera unattended.	**4** ○ 160	○ 161
5.	HDTV cameras are easier to focus than standard cameras.	**5** ○ 162	○ 163
6.	To boom up means to raise the camera pedestal.	**6** ○ 164	○ 165
7.	The drag controls on a mounting head are used to lock down the camera.	**7** ○ 166	○ 167
8.	If your camcorder has an LCD foldout monitor, you should use it to focus whenever possible because it is bigger than the viewfinder display.	**8** ○ 168	○ 169
9.	Dolly and truck movements show up as similar movements on-screen.	**9** ○ 170	○ 171
10.	A robotic pedestal is motor-driven and remotely controlled.	**10** ○ 172	○ 173
11.	The medium shot is also called a bust shot.	**11** ○ 174	○ 175
12.	Because an ENG camera can be shoulder-mounted, the operator has no need for a tripod.	**12** ○ 176	○ 177
13.	The higher the zoom ratio, the more effective the lens is for studio work.	**13** ○ 178	○ 179
14.	The handheld stabilizer is especially effective for full-sized EFP cameras.	**14** ○ 180	○ 181
15.	The jib arm and the camera crane can make the camera move in similar ways.	**15** ○ 182	○ 183
16.	Field of view refers to how far or close the object appears relative to the camera.	**16** ○ 184	○ 185
17.	Before the studio or remote production, you should check the tightest and widest field of view of the zoom lens from the principal camera position.	**17** ○ 186	○ 187
18.	Leadroom and noseroom fulfill similar framing (compositional) functions.	**18** ○ 188	○ 189

SECTION TOTAL _____

© 2012 Wadsworth, Cengage Learning

PROBLEM-SOLVING APPLICATIONS

1. Locate the pan and the tilt drag controls and the pan-and-tilt lock controls of the mounting head. Adjust them so that you can pan and tilt the camera as smoothly as necessary. When do you need to use the lock mechanism?

2. Pedestal up and down to see how high and low the camera will go. What can happen if you move the camera too fast to either end of vertical travel?

3. You are to set up a tripod on an uneven, slightly sloping field. How can you make sure that the tripod is level?

4. The director wants you to follow the new mayor up the flight of stairs in city hall without shaking the ENG/EFP camera. What camera mount would you suggest?

5. You are shooting a documentary-style program, and you don't have a tripod at the shoot. What focal length would be most effective if you want relatively steady shots? What other techniques could you consider for getting steady shots?

6. You have been asked to recommend the camera mounting equipment for a four-camera studio production. The director wants one camera to get a moving overhead shot and another camera that can physically move around the floor in a smooth arcing motion. The other two cameras will be shooting a variety of typical long shots and close-ups. Another consideration is that there will be only three camera operators available during the production. List the mounting equipment you would recommend for each camera and why.

7. During the remote coverage of the World Computer Fair, the novice director tells you to zoom in to an ECU of a laptop display and then arc the tripod dolly around the display table to show the other computers. What are the potential problems, if any?

8. In a multicamera studio dance program, the same director tells you, the operator of camera 3, that you should listen only to calls that concern your camera and ignore commands to all the other cameras. Do you agree? If so, why? If not, why not?

9. As you are leaving the studio, the producer states that a spare battery for your ENG/EFP camera is not needed because the story you are to cover will have, at best, a 20-second slot in the newscast. What is your response?

10. The producer tells you to be sure to keep enough headroom when framing an ECU. Do you agree? If so, why? If not, why not?

11. The director tells you, the camera operator, to change from an over-the-shoulder shot to a cross-shot. How can you accomplish such a shot change?

© 2012 Wadsworth, Cengage Learning

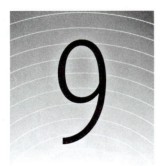

Audio: Sound Pickup

REVIEW OF KEY TERMS

Match each term with its appropriate definition by filling in the corresponding bubble.

1. unidirectional
2. flat response
3. omnidirectional
4. pickup pattern

5. polar pattern
6. condenser microphone
7. dynamic microphone
8. cardioid

9. ribbon microphone
10. impedance
11. frequency response
12. system microphone

A. A microphone whose sound pickup device consists of a thin band that vibrates with the sound pressures within a magnetic field

A
○ ○ ○ ○
1 2 3 4
○ ○ ○ ○
5 6 7 8
○ ○ ○ ○
9 10 11 12

B. A microphone whose diaphragm consists of a plate that vibrates with the sound pressure against another fixed plate (the backplate)

B
○ ○ ○ ○
1 2 3 4
○ ○ ○ ○
5 6 7 8
○ ○ ○ ○
9 10 11 12

C. A microphone that can pick up sounds better from one direction—the front—than from the sides or back

C
○ ○ ○ ○
1 2 3 4
○ ○ ○ ○
5 6 7 8
○ ○ ○ ○
9 10 11 12

P A G E
T O T A L

© 2012 Wadsworth, Cengage Learning

1. unidirectional	5. polar pattern	9. ribbon microphone	
2. flat response	6. condenser microphone	10. impedance	
3. omnidirectional	7. dynamic microphone	11. frequency response	
4. pickup pattern	8. cardioid	12. system microphone	

D. The territory around the microphone within which the microphone can "hear" well, or has optimal sound pickup

D ○ ○ ○ ○
   1 2 3 4
   ○ ○ ○ ○
   5 6 7 8
   ○ ○ ○ ○
   9 10 11 12

E. A microphone whose sound pickup device consists of a diaphragm that is attached to a movable coil

E ○ ○ ○ ○
   1 2 3 4
   ○ ○ ○ ○
   5 6 7 8
   ○ ○ ○ ○
   9 10 11 12

F. A type of resistance to a signal flow: high-Z or low-Z

F ○ ○ ○ ○
   1 2 3 4
   ○ ○ ○ ○
   5 6 7 8
   ○ ○ ○ ○
   9 10 11 12

G. The range of frequencies a microphone can hear and reproduce

G ○ ○ ○ ○
   1 2 3 4
   ○ ○ ○ ○
   5 6 7 8
   ○ ○ ○ ○
   9 10 11 12

H. A specific pickup pattern of unidirectional microphones

H ○ ○ ○ ○
   1 2 3 4
   ○ ○ ○ ○
   5 6 7 8
   ○ ○ ○ ○
   9 10 11 12

PAGE
TOTAL [   ]

© 2012 Wadsworth, Cengage Learning

I. The measure of a microphone's ability to hear equally well over its entire frequency range

I
○ ○ ○ ○
1 2 3 4
○ ○ ○ ○
5 6 7 8
○ ○ ○ ○
9 10 11 12

J. The two-dimensional representation of a microphone pickup pattern

J
○ ○ ○ ○
1 2 3 4
○ ○ ○ ○
5 6 7 8
○ ○ ○ ○
9 10 11 12

K. Uses a base and different heads for various pickup patterns

K
○ ○ ○ ○
1 2 3 4
○ ○ ○ ○
5 6 7 8
○ ○ ○ ○
9 10 11 12

L. A microphone that can pick up sounds equally well from all directions

L
○ ○ ○ ○
1 2 3 4
○ ○ ○ ○
5 6 7 8
○ ○ ○ ○
9 10 11 12

P A G E
T O T A L

S E C T I O N
T O T A L

© 2012 Wadsworth, Cengage Learning

REVIEW OF HOW MICROPHONES HEAR

1. Fill in the bubbles whose numbers correspond with the polar patterns in the figure below.

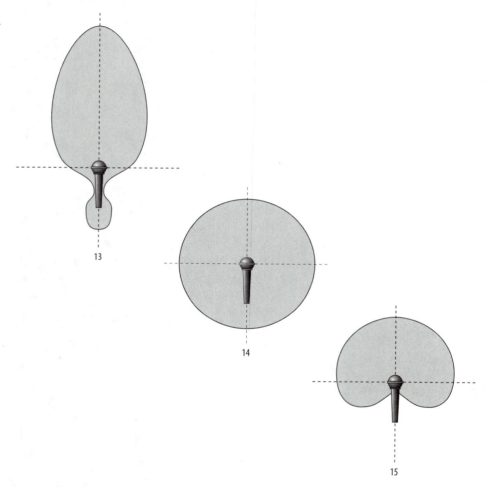

a. hypercardioid

b. cardioid

c. omnidirectional

1a ○ 13   ○ 14   ○ 15

1b ○ 13   ○ 14   ○ 15

1c ○ 13   ○ 14   ○ 15

PAGE
TOTAL ☐

© 2012 Wadsworth, Cengage Learning

Select the correct answers and fill in the bubbles with the corresponding numbers.

2. The two-dimensional representation of a microphone's sound pickup area is the (16) *safe area* (17) *polar pattern* (18) *pickup pattern*.

3. Normally, shotgun microphones have (19) *an omnidirectional* (20) *an extremely directional* (21) *a nondirectional* pickup pattern.

4. Select the three types of microphones as classified by their generating element: (22) *dynamic* (23) *unidirectional* (24) *cardioid* (25) *ribbon* (26) *condenser* (27) *hypercardioid*. **(Fill in three bubbles.)**

5. To eliminate sudden breath pops when speaking close to the microphone, we use a (28) *pop filter* (29) *windscreen* (30) *frequency filter*.

6. Microphones that require a battery or phantom power for their output signal are (31) *dynamic* (32) *ribbon* (33) *condenser*.

7. Faraway speech sounds are picked up best with (34) *a shotgun mic* (35) *an omnidirectional hand mic* (36) *a ribbon mic*.

8. The hand microphones used in ENG normally have (37) *an omnidirectional* (38) *a cardioid* (39) *a hyper- or supercardioid* pickup pattern.

9. The element in a microphone that converts sound waves into an electrical signal is the (40) *sound-generating element* (41) *sound-amplifying chip* (42) *pickup device*.

10. In general, dynamic microphones are (43) *equally sensitive as* (44) *less rugged than* (45) *more rugged than* ribbon microphones.

2	○ 16	○ 17	○ 18
3	○ 19	○ 20	○ 21
4	○ 22	○ 23	○ 24
	○ 25	○ 26	○ 27
5	○ 28	○ 29	○ 30
6	○ 31	○ 32	○ 33
7	○ 34	○ 35	○ 36
8	○ 37	○ 38	○ 39
9	○ 40	○ 41	○ 42
10	○ 43	○ 44	○ 45

PAGE TOTAL [ ]

SECTION TOTAL [ ]

© 2012 Wadsworth, Cengage Learning

REVIEW OF HOW MICROPHONES ARE USED

Select the correct answers and fill in the bubbles with the corresponding numbers.

1. The large shotgun microphone on a perambulator boom has (46) *an omnidirectional* (47) *a hyper- or supercardioid* (48) *a cardioid* pickup pattern.

2. For an optimal pickup of an acoustic guitar, you should use a (49) *dynamic* (50) *condenser* (51) *dynamic cardioid* microphone.

3. The most appropriate mics for the voice pickup of a four-member news team (two anchors, a weathercaster, and a sportscaster) are (52) *lavaliers* (53) *desk mics* (54) *boom mics*.

4. You are to set up microphones for a six-member panel discussion. All participants sit in a row at a table. Normally, you would use (55) *desk mics* (56) *hand mics* (57) *boom mics* for this production.

5. Parabolic microphones are especially effective for picking up (58) *especially soft sounds* (59) *faraway sounds* (60) *extremely close sounds*.

6. To achieve a good and efficient voice pickup during the video recording of four people sitting around a table in a small office, talking about effective sound handling in ENG/EFP, you should use a (61) *parabolic reflector mic* (62) *boundary mic* (63) *large shotgun mic*.

7. When you're setting up the mics for a panel show, the audio engineer advises you to place them in such a way that they will not cause "multiple-microphone interference." This means that the mics must be placed so that they will not (64) *block the faces of the panel members* (65) *cancel some of one another's frequencies* (66) *multiply the ambient noise*.

8. When doing a live report from an accident scene, the most practical mic is a (67) *stand mic* (68) *lavalier mic* (69) *hand mic*.

9. The sound pickup of a dramatic scene of two people sitting at the dinner table is best done with a (70) *fishpole and pencil mic* (71) *fishpole and large shotgun mic* (72) *plant mic*.

10. For miking a kick drum, the microphone that is least subject to input overload has a (73) *ribbon* (74) *condenser* (75) *dynamic* sound-generating element.

1	◯ 46	◯ 47	◯ 48
2	◯ 49	◯ 50	◯ 51
3	◯ 52	◯ 53	◯ 54
4	◯ 55	◯ 56	◯ 57
5	◯ 58	◯ 59	◯ 60
6	◯ 61	◯ 62	◯ 63
7	◯ 64	◯ 65	◯ 66
8	◯ 67	◯ 68	◯ 69
9	◯ 70	◯ 71	◯ 72
10	◯ 73	◯ 74	◯ 75

SECTION TOTAL [ ]

© 2012 Wadsworth, Cengage Learning

REVIEW QUIZ

*Mark the following statements as true or false by filling in the bubbles in the **T** (for true) or **F** (for false) column.*

	T	F

1. The pickup pattern of a system mic can be changed by attaching a different head.
   1 ○ 76 ○ 77

2. If two desk microphones are too close together, their sound pickup may be compromised by multiple-microphone interference.
   2 ○ 78 ○ 79

3. Dual redundancy refers to a backup microphone in case the first mic fails.
   3 ○ 80 ○ 81

4. Because the boundary, or pressure zone, microphone needs a sound-reflecting surface, it should not be used as a hanging mic.
   4 ○ 82 ○ 83

5. Dynamic mics are generally less sensitive to shock and temperature extremes than ribbon mics.
   5 ○ 84 ○ 85

6. Because wireless microphones operate on their own frequency, they are immune to interference from other radio frequencies.
   6 ○ 86 ○ 87

7. A windsock fulfills the identical function as a pop filter.
   7 ○ 88 ○ 89

8. A hand mic clipped to a desk stand can serve as a desk mic.
   8 ○ 90 ○ 91

9. All professional microphones use three-pronged XLR connectors.
   9 ○ 92 ○ 93

10. Blowing into a microphone is a good way to test whether it is turned on.
    10 ○ 94 ○ 95

11. Condenser mics are especially good for the pickup of a bass drum.
    11 ○ 96 ○ 97

12. Using an impedance transformer (a direct box) allows you to play an electric guitar into a mixer.
    12 ○ 98 ○ 99

13. Because lavalier microphones are highly sensitive, they work best when hidden under a shirt or blouse.
    13 ○ 100 ○ 101

14. The parabolic reflector microphone is especially appropriate for intimate, high-quality sound pickup with a high degree of sound presence.
    14 ○ 102 ○ 103

15. Lavaliers can have a dynamic or condenser sound-generating element.
    15 ○ 104 ○ 105

16. Once a microphone is turned off, it is relatively immune to physical shock.
    16 ○ 106 ○ 107

SECTION TOTAL [   ]

© 2012 Wadsworth, Cengage Learning

PROBLEM-SOLVING APPLICATIONS

1. You are responsible for the audio pickup of the live remote coverage at the airport during the Thanksgiving rush. Basically, you will have a reporter walking among the people waiting at the ticket counters, briefly interviewing some of the travelers. What type of mic would you use? Why?

2. You are in charge of audio for a show that consists of several intimate numbers by a singer and a small band. After the rehearsal an observer in the control room tells you that the singer holds the mic much too close to her mouth and that she should hold the mic lower and sing *across* rather than *into* it. What is your reaction? Why?

3. You are to provide optimal sound pickup for a preschool children's live-recorded show. The show consists of a host who moves among five to seven children seated on little chairs. The chairs are grouped around a small rug on which the children also play or dance from time to time. The dance music and other recorded audio portions are piped into the studio through the S.A. system. What microphone setup would you suggest for the host and the children? What problems might the S.A. system cause, if any?

4. An official at your former high school asks you to help with the audio for the championship basketball game. Somehow, so the official claims, the visiting spectators seem much louder on television than the home audience, although the latter is actually much larger and noisier than the guests. What can you do to accurately reflect the supportive cheering of the two sides? What specific microphone setups would you use?

5. You are doing a documentary on police patrols in your city. You first want to hear the conversation and the police radio inside the patrol car and then capture the sounds of conversations, yelling, or any other audio when the officers leave the patrol car to confront a suspect. What microphones would you need for optimal sound pickup in these situations?

6. You are to conduct an interview with the university president in her office. What microphones would you use? Why?

7. You are responsible for the pickup of an important live interview with a famous musician. The TD urges you to be sure to have an effective backup in case one of your lavalier mics fails. What is the easiest way to do this?

© 2012 Wadsworth, Cengage Learning

Audio: Sound Control

REVIEW OF KEY TERMS

Match each term with its appropriate definition by filling in the corresponding bubble.

1. digital audiotape
2. sound perspective
3. ambience
4. automatic gain control

5. mix-minus
6. equalization
7. sweetening
8. VU meter

9. calibrate
10. figure/ground
11. MP3
12. mixing

A. A common codec for digital audio

A ○ ○ ○ ○
    1 2 3 4
   ○ ○ ○ ○
    5 6 7 8
   ○ ○ ○ ○
    9 10 11 12

B. Emphasizing the most important sound source over other sounds

B ○ ○ ○ ○
    1 2 3 4
   ○ ○ ○ ○
    5 6 7 8
   ○ ○ ○ ○
    9 10 11 12

C. A variety of quality adjustments of recorded sound in postproduction

C ○ ○ ○ ○
    1 2 3 4
   ○ ○ ○ ○
    5 6 7 8
   ○ ○ ○ ○
    9 10 11 12

PAGE
TOTAL [ ]

© 2012 Wadsworth, Cengage Learning

1. digital audiotape	5. mix-minus	9. calibrate
2. sound perspective	6. equalization	10. figure/ground
3. ambience	7. sweetening	11. MP3
4. automatic gain control	8. VU meter	12. mixing

D. Regulates the audio or video levels automatically, without using pots

D
1 2 3 4
5 6 7 8
9 10 11 12

E. Controlling the audio signal by emphasizing certain frequencies and eliminating others

E
1 2 3 4
5 6 7 8
9 10 11 12

F. Combining two or more sounds in specific proportions as determined by the event context

F
1 2 3 4
5 6 7 8
9 10 11 12

G. Far sounds go with long shots; close sounds with close-ups

G
1 2 3 4
5 6 7 8
9 10 11 12

H. Making all VU meters respond in the same way to a specific audio signal

H
1 2 3 4
5 6 7 8
9 10 11 12

PAGE
TOTAL

© 2012 Wadsworth, Cengage Learning

I. Encodes and records sound signals in digital form

I.
○ ○ ○ ○
1 2 3 4
○ ○ ○ ○
5 6 7 8
○ ○ ○ ○
9 10 11 12

J. Measures the relative loudness of sound

J.
○ ○ ○ ○
1 2 3 4
○ ○ ○ ○
5 6 7 8
○ ○ ○ ○
9 10 11 12

K. Type of multiple audio feed missing the part that is being recorded

K.
○ ○ ○ ○
1 2 3 4
○ ○ ○ ○
5 6 7 8
○ ○ ○ ○
9 10 11 12

L. Environmental sounds

L.
○ ○ ○ ○
1 2 3 4
○ ○ ○ ○
5 6 7 8
○ ○ ○ ○
9 10 11 12

PAGE TOTAL _____

SECTION TOTAL _____

© 2012 Wadsworth, Cengage Learning

REVIEW OF STUDIO AND FIELD AUDIO PRODUCTION EQUIPMENT

Select the correct answers and fill in the bubbles with the corresponding numbers.

1. A television audio console lets you (13) *synchronize audio and video in postproduction* (14) *punch up the audio source with the corresponding video* (15) *adjust the volume of each audio input.*

2. All professional video-editing systems let you control and mix (16) *only one audio track* (17) *two or more audio tracks* (18) *no audio tracks unless you interface it with special audio software.*

3. The trim control on the modules of studio consoles regulates the strength of the (19) *outgoing audio signal* (20) *final mix* (21) *incoming audio signal.*

4. The appropriate place that marks the beginning of the "overload zone" is (22) *–5 VU* (23) *–2 VU* (24) *0 VU.*

1	○ 13	○ 14	○ 15
2	○ 16	○ 17	○ 18
3	○ 19	○ 20	○ 21
4	○ 22	○ 23	○ 24

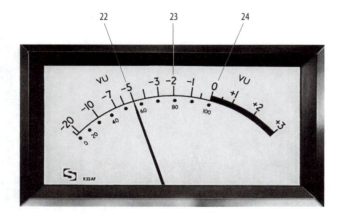

PAGE TOTAL

PHOTO: SELCO PRODUCTS CO.

© 2012 Wadsworth, Cengage Learning

5. Fill in the bubble whose number identifies the type of head in the head assembly below:

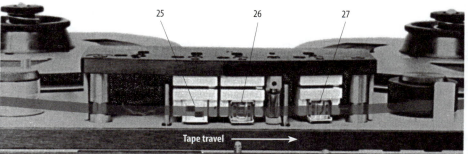

25   26   27

Tape travel ⟶

a. playback head

b. record head

c. erase head

6. Most professional video- and sound-editing software lets you (28) *only see* (29) *only hear* (30) *both see and hear* the audio track.

7. A 16 × 2 audio console has (31) *16 inputs and 2 outputs* (32) *16 slide faders and 2 monitor systems* (33) *16 VU meters and 2 mix buses.*

8. Phantom power means that the power is (34) *virtual but not real* (35) *not necessary* (36) *not supplied by battery but by some other source.*

9. When an incoming mic signal is routed to the mic-level input, it (37) *will be distorted* (38) *must be amplified* (39) *will sound just right.*

10. The equalization controls on console modules (40) *bring all sounds to the same volume level* (41) *emphasize or de-emphasize certain frequencies* (42) *bring all incoming sounds to line-level strength.*

11. The advantage of memory cards over a DAT recorder is that they (43) *have no moving parts* (44) *can store digital and analog audio signals* (45) *can record MP3.*

12. The advantage of hard disks over a DAT recorder is that the audio information can be (46) *digital* (47) *analog or digital* (48) *accessed randomly.*

5a	○ 25	○ 26	○ 27
5b	○ 25	○ 26	○ 27
5c	○ 25	○ 26	○ 27
6	○ 28	○ 29	○ 30
7	○ 31	○ 32	○ 33
8	○ 34	○ 35	○ 36
9	○ 37	○ 38	○ 39
10	○ 40	○ 41	○ 42
11	○ 43	○ 44	○ 45
12	○ 46	○ 47	○ 48

PAGE TOTAL [ ]

SECTION TOTAL [ ]

PHOTO: WILLIAM STORM

© 2012 Wadsworth, Cengage Learning

Select the correct answers and fill in the bubbles with the corresponding numbers.

1. Audio-system calibration normally refers to (49) *adjusting the audio input VU meter of the VR to the VU meter of the console output* (50) *adjusting the zoom lens so that it stays in focus* (51) *having the VU meter of the VR peak at a much higher level than the VU meter of the console output.*

| 1 | ○ 49 | ○ 50 | ○ 51 |

2. The proper steps for audio system calibration are:

| 2 | ○ 52 | ○ 53 | ○ 54 |

    (52) *1. Activate the control tone on the console or mixer.*
         2. Turn up the volume control for the incoming sound on the VR to 0 VU.
         3. Bring up the control tone fader on the console or mixer to 0 VU.
         4. Bring up the master fader on the console or mixer to 0 VU.

    (53) *1. Turn up the volume control for the incoming sound on the VR to 0 VU.*
         2. Bring up the control tone fader on the console or mixer to 0 VU.
         3. Bring up the master fader on the console or mixer to 0 VU.
         4. Activate the control tone on the console or mixer.

    (54) *1. Activate the control tone on the console or mixer.*
         2. Bring up the master fader on the console or mixer to 0 VU.
         3. Bring up the control tone fader on the console or mixer to 0 VU.
         4. Turn up the volume control for the incoming sound on the VR to 0 VU.

3. When using a CD player as an additional audio source, it must be connected to the (55) *mic* (56) *line* (57) *neither the mic nor the line* input on the mixer.

| 3 | ○ 55 | ○ 56 | ○ 57 |

4. The audio control tone, which gives a reference level of the recorded material, should be set at (58) *0 VU* (59) *+3 VU* (60) *−3 VU.*

| 4 | ○ 58 | ○ 59 | ○ 60 |

5. The AGC (61) *discriminates automatically between figure and ground* (62) *works especially well in noisy surroundings* (63) *automatically boosts audio levels if they fall below preset levels.*

| 5 | ○ 61 | ○ 62 | ○ 63 |

6. When recording sound during an outdoor EFP, you should (64) *avoid all ambient sounds* (65) *record ambient sounds on a separate track* (66) *re-create the ambient sounds in postproduction.*

| 6 | ○ 64 | ○ 65 | ○ 66 |

P A G E
T O T A L [ ]

© 2012 Wadsworth, Cengage Learning

7. The correct patches as shown in the figure are: (67) (68) (69) (70) (71) (72).
(Multiple answers are possible.)

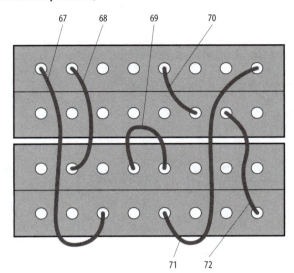

8. A memory card can store (73) *only analog* (74) *only digital* (75) *both analog and digital* audio signals.

9. Indicate the most common place to cut the digital audio track shown below.

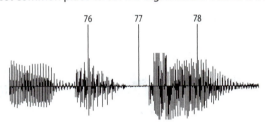

10. Taking a level is (79) *not necessary when the AGC is engaged* (80) *not necessary when recording digital sound* (81) *always necessary.*

11. The least critical speaker placement in a 5.1 surround-sound system is the (82) *front-center speaker* (83) *front-side speakers* (84) *subwoofer.*

12. Recording several minutes of room tone or ambient field sounds during a field production is especially important for (85) *establishing continuity in postproduction* (86) *helping set volume levels in postproduction* (87) *boosting aesthetic energy.*

7 ○ 67 ○ 68 ○ 69
     ○ 70 ○ 71 ○ 72

8 ○ 73 ○ 74 ○ 75

9 ○ 76 ○ 77 ○ 78

10 ○ 79 ○ 80 ○ 81

11 ○ 82 ○ 83 ○ 84

12 ○ 85 ○ 86 ○ 87

PAGE TOTAL [ ]

SECTION TOTAL [ ]

© 2012 Wadsworth, Cengage Learning

Mark the following statements as true or false by filling in the bubbles in the **T** (for true) or **F** (for false) column.

		T	F
1.	The VU meter or the PPM will give an accurate reading of sound perspective.	◯ 88	◯ 89
2.	The .1 speaker in the 5.1 surround sound system is the subwoofer.	◯ 90	◯ 91
3.	Environmental sounds are always interfering in EFP.	◯ 92	◯ 93
4.	All analog recording systems are tape-based.	◯ 94	◯ 95
5.	In EFP we should try to mix all sound inputs as much as possible to minimize the need for postproduction mixing.	◯ 96	◯ 97
6.	I/O consoles have an output channel for each input channel.	◯ 98	◯ 99
7.	On large multichannel consoles, each input channel has its own quality controls.	◯ 100	◯ 101
8.	In contrast to large audio consoles, audio mixers have only one input but several outputs.	◯ 102	◯ 103
9.	Small digital stereo recorders use an SD memory card for the storage of audio signals.	◯ 104	◯ 105
10.	Digital audio signals can be recorded on tape or computer disks.	◯ 106	◯ 107
11.	An audio field mixer has quality controls similar to those of a console.	◯ 108	◯ 109
12.	One function of the audio console is to route the combined signals to a specific output.	◯ 110	◯ 111
13.	When recording digital audio, the master fader level should be kept somewhat below 0 VU.	◯ 112	◯ 113
14.	A flat response means that the dynamics are equalized.	◯ 114	◯ 115
15.	DAT recorders allow random access.	◯ 116	◯ 117
16.	Adding rhythmic sound is one of the primary techniques for establishing visual continuity.	◯ 118	◯ 119
17.	A solo switch on the console lets you listen to a single incoming sound while silencing all others.	◯ 120	◯ 121

SECTION TOTAL [ ]

© 2012 Wadsworth, Cengage Learning

PROBLEM-SOLVING APPLICATIONS

1. When setting up for video-recording a small rock group, you notice that the microphones and other audio sources exceed the number of inputs on the audio console. What can you do?

2. During rehearsal of the same production, you discover that the audio inputs that need the most attention are widely spread apart on the board. How can you get them closer together on the console so that their respective volume controls are adjacent to one another?

3. During a small segment of an EFP in an auto assembly plant, the novice director tells you to be especially careful to mix the ambient sounds and the voices of the reporter and the plant supervisor with the portable mixer so as to facilitate postproduction editing. What is your response?

4. During the digital recording of a concert, the VU meters occasionally peak into the +2 red zone. The director is very concerned about overmodulation. What is your response?

5. Some of the incoming audio signals during a rock concert are so hot (strong) that they bend the needle even at very low fader settings. What can you do to correct this problem without adjusting the source?

6. You have been asked to calibrate the audio system in your studio. Briefly describe the process step-by-step.

7. The director of the evening news would like you, the audio technician, to construct a playlist of all the bumpers for an automated and sequenced playback during the newscast. What piece of widely used audio equipment do you need to accomplish this assignment?

8. You, the audio technician, overhear the floor manager telling the anchorpersons that they do not need to be on the I.F.B. system because it is, after all, his job to relay messages to the talent. What is your response?

9. How can you control the input levels before they reach the camcorder?

10. During postproduction the director insists on laying in a low but highly rhythmical music track, even under the dialogue, to boost the aesthetic energy of the scene. What is your reaction?

© 2012 Wadsworth, Cengage Learning

Lighting

REVIEW OF KEY TERMS

Match each term with its appropriate definition by filling in the corresponding bubble.

1. ND filter
2. baselight
3. softlight
4. reflected light
5. incident light

6. cookie
7. foot-candle
8. lumen
9. dimmer
10. floodlight

11. fluorescent
12. spotlight
13. incandescent
14. lux
15. barn doors

A. A lighting instrument that produces diffused light with a relatively undefined beam edge

A ○1 ○2 ○3 ○4 ○5
   ○6 ○7 ○8 ○9 ○10
   ○11 ○12 ○13 ○14 ○15

B. Light that is bounced off the illuminated object

B ○1 ○2 ○3 ○4 ○5
   ○6 ○7 ○8 ○9 ○10
   ○11 ○12 ○13 ○14 ○15

C. A lighting instrument that produces directional, relatively undiffused light

C ○1 ○2 ○3 ○4 ○5
   ○6 ○7 ○8 ○9 ○10
   ○11 ○12 ○13 ○14 ○15

PAGE TOTAL [   ]

© 2012 Wadsworth, Cengage Learning

1. ND filter	6. cookie	11. fluorescent
2. baselight	7. foot-candle	12. spotlight
3. softlight	8. lumen	13. incandescent
4. reflected light	9. dimmer	14. lux
5. incident light	10. floodlight	15. barn doors

D. Even, nondirectional (diffused) light necessary for the camera to operate optimally

D
○ ○ ○ ○ ○
1 2 3 4 5
○ ○ ○ ○ ○
6 7 8 9 10
○ ○ ○ ○ ○
11 12 13 14 15

E. Metal flaps in front of lighting instruments that control the spread of the light beam

E
○ ○ ○ ○ ○
1 2 3 4 5
○ ○ ○ ○ ○
6 7 8 9 10
○ ○ ○ ○ ○
11 12 13 14 15

F. A metal cutout for a pattern projection

F
○ ○ ○ ○ ○
1 2 3 4 5
○ ○ ○ ○ ○
6 7 8 9 10
○ ○ ○ ○ ○
11 12 13 14 15

G. Light that strikes the object directly from its source

G
○ ○ ○ ○ ○
1 2 3 4 5
○ ○ ○ ○ ○
6 7 8 9 10
○ ○ ○ ○ ○
11 12 13 14 15

H. The American unit of measurement of illumination, or the amount of light that falls on an object

H
○ ○ ○ ○ ○
1 2 3 4 5
○ ○ ○ ○ ○
6 7 8 9 10
○ ○ ○ ○ ○
11 12 13 14 15

PAGE
TOTAL

© 2012 Wadsworth, Cengage Learning

I. Light produced by a glowing tungsten filament

I	○ 1	○ 2	○ 3	○ 4	○ 5
	○ 6	○ 7	○ 8	○ 9	○ 10
	○ 11	○ 12	○ 13	○ 14	○ 15

J. The intensity of one candle (or any other light source radiating isotropically)

J	○ 1	○ 2	○ 3	○ 4	○ 5
	○ 6	○ 7	○ 8	○ 9	○ 10
	○ 11	○ 12	○ 13	○ 14	○ 15

K. Lamps that generate light by activating a gas-filled tube

K	○ 1	○ 2	○ 3	○ 4	○ 5
	○ 6	○ 7	○ 8	○ 9	○ 10
	○ 11	○ 12	○ 13	○ 14	○ 15

L. European standard for measuring light intensity

L	○ 1	○ 2	○ 3	○ 4	○ 5
	○ 6	○ 7	○ 8	○ 9	○ 10
	○ 11	○ 12	○ 13	○ 14	○ 15

M. Floodlight that produces extremely diffused light

M	○ 1	○ 2	○ 3	○ 4	○ 5
	○ 6	○ 7	○ 8	○ 9	○ 10
	○ 11	○ 12	○ 13	○ 14	○ 15

N. A device that controls light intensity

N	○ 1	○ 2	○ 3	○ 4	○ 5
	○ 6	○ 7	○ 8	○ 9	○ 10
	○ 11	○ 12	○ 13	○ 14	○ 15

P A G E
T O T A L [   ]

© 2012 Wadsworth, Cengage Learning

2. You can make a fluorescent light beam somewhat directional by attaching (22) *an egg crate* (23) *a filter* (24) *barn doors.*

3. Scoops have (25) *a Fresnel lens* (26) *a plain lens* (27) *no lens.*

4. A dimmer controls the (28) *voltage flowing to the lamp* (29) *wattage of the lamp* (30) *amperes flowing to the lamp.*

5. To flood (spread) the light beam of a Fresnel spotlight, you need to move the lamp-reflector unit (31) *toward* (32) *away from* the lens.

6. With the use of the patchboard (or computer patching), you (33) *must link only one instrument* (34) *can link several instruments* (35) *must link all available instruments simultaneously* to a specific dimmer.

7. Fill in the bubbles whose numbers correspond with the appropriate lighting instruments shown below.

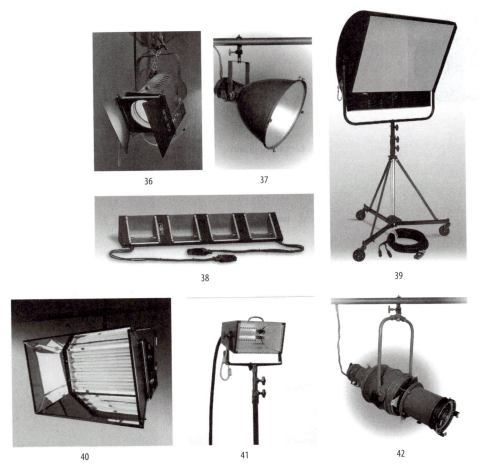

36

37

38

39

40

41

42

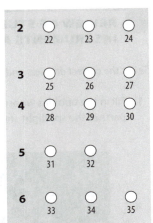

2	○ 22	○ 23	○ 24
3	○ 25	○ 26	○ 27
4	○ 28	○ 29	○ 30
5	○ 31	○ 32	
6	○ 33	○ 34	○ 35

PAGE TOTAL

PHOTO 36: HERBERT ZETTL.

PHOTOS 37, 38, 39, 41 & 42: MOLE-RICHARDSON CO.

PHOTO 40: LOWEL-LIGHT MFG., INC.

© 2012 Wadsworth, Cengage Learning

a. strip, or cyc, light

7a	○ 36	○ 37	○ 38	○ 39

7a ○ 36 ○ 37 ○ 38 ○ 39
      ○ 40 ○ 41 ○ 42

b. fluorescent floodlight bank

7b ○ 36 ○ 37 ○ 38 ○ 39
      ○ 40 ○ 41 ○ 42

c. Fresnel spotlight

7c ○ 36 ○ 37 ○ 38 ○ 39
      ○ 40 ○ 41 ○ 42

d. scoop

7d ○ 36 ○ 37 ○ 38 ○ 39
      ○ 40 ○ 41 ○ 42

e. ellipsoidal spotlight

7e ○ 36 ○ 37 ○ 38 ○ 39
      ○ 40 ○ 41 ○ 42

f. softlight

7f ○ 36 ○ 37 ○ 38 ○ 39
      ○ 40 ○ 41 ○ 42

g. broad

7g ○ 36 ○ 37 ○ 38 ○ 39
      ○ 40 ○ 41 ○ 42

8. To diffuse the light beam of a scoop even more, you can attach (43) *an egg crate* (44) *a scrim* (45) *color media.*

8 ○ 43   ○ 44   ○ 45

9. The beam of softlights can be adjusted by (46) *an egg crate* (47) *a focus control* (48) *moving the lamp assembly toward or away from the reflector.*

9 ○ 46   ○ 47   ○ 48

P A G E
T O T A L [   ]

SECTION
T O T A L [   ]

© 2012 Wadsworth, Cengage Learning

REVIEW OF FIELD LIGHTING INSTRUMENTS AND CONTROLS

Select the correct answers and fill in the bubbles with the corresponding numbers.

1. The diffusion umbrella fulfills a similar function to (49) *a dimmer* (50) *a soft box* (51) *barn doors.*

2. The easiest way to reduce the light intensity of a portable spot is to (52) *use a small dimmer* (53) *use a smaller lamp* (54) *move the light farther away from the object.*

3. One common way to diffuse the light of an open-face spot is to (55) *attach a scrim to the barn doors* (56) *attach color media* (57) *use a dimmer.*

4. Portable light stands must always be secured with (58) *a safety cable* (59) *sandbags* (60) *counterweights.*

5. Fill in the bubbles whose numbers correspond with the appropriate instruments shown below.

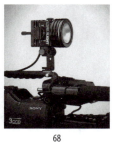
61

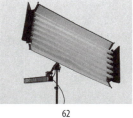
62

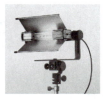
63

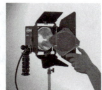
64

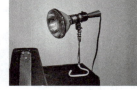
65

66

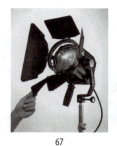
67

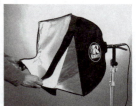
68

1	○ 49	○ 50	○ 51
2	○ 52	○ 53	○ 54
3	○ 55	○ 56	○ 57
4	○ 58	○ 59	○ 60

PAGE
TOTAL

PHOTOS 61, 62, 64, 66, 67 & 68: LOWEL-LIGHT MFG., INC.

PHOTO 63: CHIMERA

PHOTO 65: HERBERT ZETTL

© 2012 Wadsworth, Cengage Learning

a. Chinese lantern

5a ○ ○ ○ ○
　　61　62　63　64
　　○ ○ ○ ○
　　65　66　67　68

b. open-face spot

5b ○ ○ ○ ○
　　61　62　63　64
　　○ ○ ○ ○
　　65　66　67　68

c. portable fluorescent

5c ○ ○ ○ ○
　　61　62　63　64
　　○ ○ ○ ○
　　65　66　67　68

d. internal reflector light

5d ○ ○ ○ ○
　　61　62　63　64
　　○ ○ ○ ○
　　65　66　67　68

e. camera light

5e ○ ○ ○ ○
　　61　62　63　64
　　○ ○ ○ ○
　　65　66　67　68

f. soft box

5f ○ ○ ○ ○
　　61　62　63　64
　　○ ○ ○ ○
　　65　66　67　68

g. V-light

5g ○ ○ ○ ○
　　61　62　63　64
　　○ ○ ○ ○
　　65　66　67　68

h. small Fresnel spot

5h ○ ○ ○ ○
　　61　62　63　64
　　○ ○ ○ ○
　　65　66　67　68

PAGE TOTAL [　　　]

SECTION TOTAL [　　　]

© 2012 Wadsworth, Cengage Learning

REVIEW OF LIGHT INTENSITY, LAMPS, AND COLOR MEDIA

Select the correct answers and fill in the bubbles with the corresponding numbers.

1. One foot-candle is approximately (69) *10* (70) *100 lux* (71) *1.*

2. When measuring baselight, you need to read (72) *incident* (73) *reflected* (74) *directional light.*

3. When measuring incident light, you point the foot-candle or lux meter (75) *toward the set* (76) *toward the camera lens* (77) *close to the lighted object.*

4. When reading reflected light, you point the light meter (78) *into the lights* (79) *close to the lighted object* (80) *toward the camera lens.*

5. The beam of softlights (81) *can be adjusted by moving the lamp-reflector unit toward or away from the reflector* (82) *can be adjusted by attaching a Fresnel lens* (83) *cannot be sharply focused.*

6. To flood (spread) the light beam of a Fresnel spotlight, you need to move the lamp-reflector unit (84) *away from* (85) *toward* the lens.

7. Colors are frequently distorted by (86) *inadequate baselight levels* (87) *low-contrast lighting* (88) *lack of shadows.*

8. Quartz lamps fall into the (89) *fluorescent* (90) *incandescent* (91) *HMI* category.

9. The advantage of a quartz lamp is that it (92) *burns at a lower temperature* (93) *does not change color temperature over time* (94) *will not burn out over time.*

10. When aiming a colored light beam on a colored object, they (95) *mix additively* (96) *mix subtractively* (97) *do not mix.*

11. When aiming two different-colored light beams on a neutral-colored background area, they (98) *mix additively* (99) *mix subtractively* (100) *do not mix.*

12. Most fluorescent tubes (101) *burn at exactly 3,200K and 5,600K* (102) *approximate the indoor and outdoor color temperature standards* (103) *do not burn with a color temperature at all.*

13. When putting a red and a green color media in front of the same instrument, you will (104) *generate a yellow light beam* (105) *generate a cool red beam* (106) *block all light coming from the instrument.*

1 ○ 69	○ 70	○ 71
2 ○ 72	○ 73	○ 74
3 ○ 75	○ 76	○ 77
4 ○ 78	○ 79	○ 80
5 ○ 81	○ 82	○ 83
6 ○ 84	○ 85	
7 ○ 86	○ 87	○ 88
8 ○ 89	○ 90	○ 91
9 ○ 92	○ 93	○ 94
10 ○ 95	○ 96	○ 97
11 ○ 98	○ 99	○ 100
12 ○ 101	○ 102	○ 103
13 ○ 104	○ 105	○ 106

SECTION TOTAL

© 2012 Wadsworth, Cengage Learning

▮ REVIEW QUIZ

*Mark the following statements as true or false by filling in the bubbles in the **T** (for true) or*
***F** (for false) column.*

		T	F

1. A sliding rod and pantograph fulfill similar functions.

1 ○ 107 ○ 108

2. Focusing a light results in sharper shadows.

2 ○ 109 ○ 110

3. Barn doors are primarily used for intensity control.

3 ○ 111 ○ 112

4. To illuminate a large area with even light, we use a variety of Fresnel spots.

4 ○ 113 ○ 114

5. Portable fluorescent banks are used to illuminate areas with even light.

5 ○ 115 ○ 116

6. You can use egg crates to further soften the beam of softlights.

6 ○ 117 ○ 118

7. The shutters on an ellipsoidal spot can shape its beam.

7 ○ 119 ○ 120

8. One effective method of turning a spotlight into a floodlight is to shine its beam into a diffusion umbrella.

8 ○ 121 ○ 122

9. Incident light can be measured by pointing the light meter into the lights or toward the camera lens.

9 ○ 123 ○ 124

10. Regardless of the type of dimmer control, all patching must be done with patch cords for each instrument.

10 ○ 125 ○ 126

11. An HMI light needs an external ballast to function.

11 ○ 127 ○ 128

12. When necessary, the beam of softlights can be focused.

12 ○ 129 ○ 130

13. LED lights can be used to illuminate small areas for close-ups.

13 ○ 131 ○ 132

14. A flag has a similar function to barn doors.

14 ○ 133 ○ 134

15. LED lights throw a sharp light beam.

15 ○ 135 ○ 136

16. The inverse square law is independent of how much the light is collimated.

16 ○ 137 ○ 138

17. A reflector can substitute for a fill light.

17 ○ 139 ○ 140

PAGE
TOTAL ▭

SECTION
TOTAL ▭

© 2012 Wadsworth, Cengage Learning

PROBLEM-SOLVING APPLICATIONS

1. You are asked to raise the baselight level in a classroom for optimal camera performance. Even though the small portable spotlights are in the maximum flood position, the additional illumination is not even. What other methods do you have available to achieve further diffusion?

2. You are asked to produce extremely sharp beams that reflect as precise pools of light on the studio floor. What type of lighting instruments would you use?

3. When checking the general baselight level and the amount of foot-candles (or lux) falling on the subject, the lighting assistant first stands next to the lighted subject and points the light meter toward the principal camera position. Will the assistant's action produce the desired results? If so, why? If not, why not?

4. You are asked to assemble a lighting kit that will be useful for lighting indoor interviews in small rooms, such as hotel rooms and offices. What instruments and other necessary equipment would you recommend?

5. You are asked to dim all spotlights simultaneously and then do the same thing immediately thereafter with all floodlights. How can you best accomplish this task?

6. The producer asked you to shine a yellow light on a blue commercial display to make one side look "greenish." What is your reaction?

7. The basketball coach of the local high school asks the television production teacher to flood the gym with HMI lights. What are your concerns, if any?

8. When video-recording a commercial for a local jewelry store, you are asked by the owner to try LED lights for illuminating a diamond ring because he wants a minimum of shadows. What is your reaction?

© 2012 Wadsworth, Cengage Learning

12 Techniques of Television Lighting

REVIEW OF KEY TERMS

Match each term with its appropriate definition by filling in the corresponding bubble.

1. **photographic lighting principle**
2. **side light**
3. **key light**
4. **light plot**

5. **fill light**
6. **cameo lighting**
7. **floor plan**
8. **falloff**
9. **background light**

10. **kicker light**
11. **low-key**
12. **silhouette lighting**
13. **high-key**
14. **back light**

A. Illuminates the set, set pieces, and backdrops

A
○ ○ ○ ○ ○
1 2 3 4 5
○ ○ ○ ○ ○
6 7 8 9 10
○ ○ ○ ○
11 12 13 14

B. Dark background, with a few selective light sources on the scene

B
○ ○ ○ ○ ○
1 2 3 4 5
○ ○ ○ ○ ○
6 7 8 9 10
○ ○ ○ ○
11 12 13 14

C. Illumination from behind and above the subject and opposite the camera

C
○ ○ ○ ○ ○
1 2 3 4 5
○ ○ ○ ○ ○
6 7 8 9 10
○ ○ ○ ○
11 12 13 14

PAGE
TOTAL [   ]

© 2012 Wadsworth, Cengage Learning

1. photographic lighting principle	5. fill light	10. kicker light
2. side light	6. cameo lighting	11. low-key
3. key light	7. floor plan	12. silhouette lighting
4. light plot	8. falloff	13. high-key
	9. background light	14. back light

D. The speed with which a light picture portion turns into shadow area

D ① ② ③ ④ ⑤ (1 2 3 4 5)
⑥ ⑦ ⑧ ⑨ ⑩ (6 7 8 9 10)
⑪ ⑫ ⑬ ⑭ (11 12 13 14)

E. Unlighted subject in front of a brightly illuminated background

E ① ② ③ ④ ⑤ (1 2 3 4 5)
⑥ ⑦ ⑧ ⑨ ⑩ (6 7 8 9 10)
⑪ ⑫ ⑬ ⑭ (11 12 13 14)

F. Light background and ample light on the scene

F ① ② ③ ④ ⑤ (1 2 3 4 5)
⑥ ⑦ ⑧ ⑨ ⑩ (6 7 8 9 10)
⑪ ⑫ ⑬ ⑭ (11 12 13 14)

G. The triangular arrangement of the three major light sources used to illuminate a subject

G ① ② ③ ④ ⑤ (1 2 3 4 5)
⑥ ⑦ ⑧ ⑨ ⑩ (6 7 8 9 10)
⑪ ⑫ ⑬ ⑭ (11 12 13 14)

H. Lighted subject in front of a dark background

H ① ② ③ ④ ⑤ (1 2 3 4 5)
⑥ ⑦ ⑧ ⑨ ⑩ (6 7 8 9 10)
⑪ ⑫ ⑬ ⑭ (11 12 13 14)

PAGE TOTAL ☐

© 2012 Wadsworth, Cengage Learning

I. Additional light that illuminates shadow areas and thereby reduces falloff

I ○ ○ ○ ○ ○
   1 2 3 4 5
   ○ ○ ○ ○ ○
   6 7 8 9 10
   ○ ○ ○ ○
   11 12 13 14

J. Principal source of illumination

J ○ ○ ○ ○ ○
   1 2 3 4 5
   ○ ○ ○ ○ ○
   6 7 8 9 10
   ○ ○ ○ ○
   11 12 13 14

K. A plan that shows each lighting instrument used relative to the scene to be lighted

K ○ ○ ○ ○ ○
   1 2 3 4 5
   ○ ○ ○ ○ ○
   6 7 8 9 10
   ○ ○ ○ ○
   11 12 13 14

L. Directional light from the side of an object

L ○ ○ ○ ○ ○
   1 2 3 4 5
   ○ ○ ○ ○ ○
   6 7 8 9 10
   ○ ○ ○ ○
   11 12 13 14

M. Directional light coming from the side and the back of the subject, usually from below

M ○ ○ ○ ○ ○
   1 2 3 4 5
   ○ ○ ○ ○ ○
   6 7 8 9 10
   ○ ○ ○ ○
   11 12 13 14

N. A diagram of scenery and major properties drawn onto a grid

N ○ ○ ○ ○ ○
   1 2 3 4 5
   ○ ○ ○ ○ ○
   6 7 8 9 10
   ○ ○ ○ ○
   11 12 13 14

PAGE
TOTAL [ ]

SECTION
TOTAL [ ]

W-141

© 2012 Wadsworth, Cengage Learning

c.

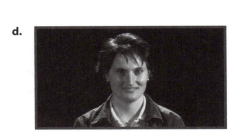

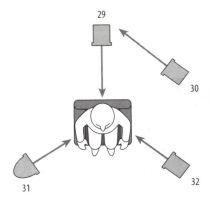

29

30

31 32

Camera

PHOTO: EDWARD AIONA

3c ○ ○ ○ ○
29 30 31 32

d.

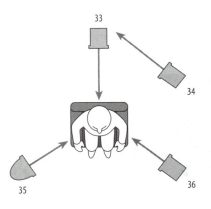

33

34

35 36

Camera

PHOTO: EDWARD AIONA

3d ○ ○ ○ ○
33 34 35 36

P A G E
T O T A L

© 2012 Wadsworth, Cengage Learning

4. You are to evaluate normal lighting setups. In the following six figures, cross out the lighting instruments that are unnecessary or most likely to interfere with the intended lighting effects; then fill in the bubbles whose numbers correspond with the instruments *needed*.

a. cameo lighting

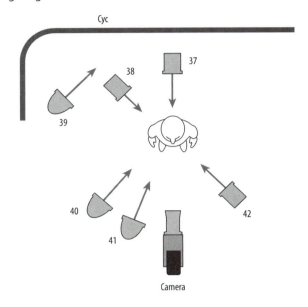

Cyc

Camera

b. small still-life lighting

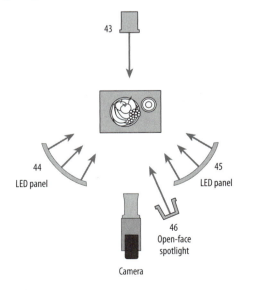

43

LED panel 44   45 LED panel

46
Open-face
spotlight

Camera

4a ○ 37   ○ 38   ○ 39
        ○ 40   ○ 41   ○ 42

4b ○ 43 ○ 44 ○ 45 ○ 46

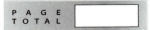

P A G E
T O T A L [   ]

© 2012 Wadsworth, Cengage Learning

c. chroma-key-area lighting

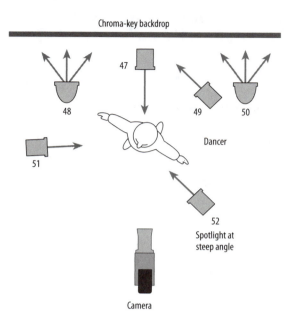

Chroma-key backdrop

47

48   49   50

Dancer

51

52
Spotlight at
steep angle

Camera

d. newscast

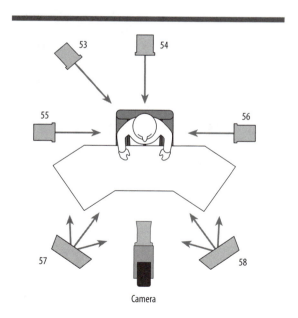

53   54

55   56

57   58

Camera

4c ○ 47 ○ 48 ○ 49
  ○ 50 ○ 51 ○ 52

4d ○ 53 ○ 54 ○ 55
  ○ 56 ○ 57 ○ 58

P A G E
T O T A L

© 2012 Wadsworth, Cengage Learning

e. speaker and audience

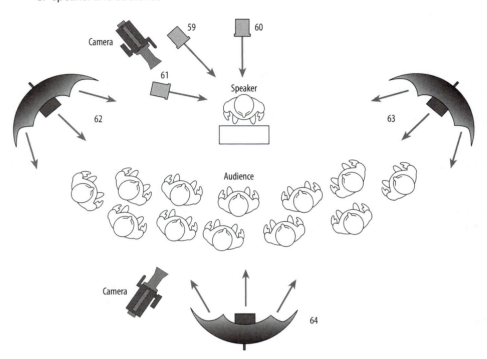

Camera
59
60
61
62
Speaker
63
Audience
Camera
64

f. dancer in silhouette

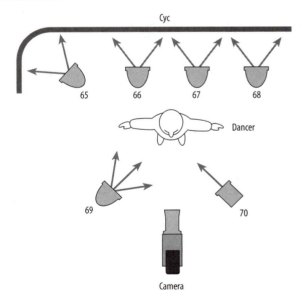

Cyc
65   66   67   68
Dancer
69   70
Camera

4e ○ 59 ○ 60 ○ 61
     ○ 62 ○ 63 ○ 64

4f ○ 65 ○ 66 ○ 67
     ○ 68 ○ 69 ○ 70

PAGE
TOTAL

© 2012 Wadsworth, Cengage Learning

5. Excessive dimming of incandescent lights (more than 10 percent of full power) will (71) *not affect* (72) *decrease* (73) *increase* the color temperature. This means that the white light will (74) *remain basically unchanged* (75) *turn reddish* (76) *turn bluish*. **(Fill in two bubbles.)**

5	○ 71	○ 72	○ 73
	○ 74	○ 75	○ 76

6. To figure the total wattage that a circuit can safely carry, you should multiply the number of amps by (77) *15* (78) *75* (79) *100*.

6	○ 77	○ 78	○ 79

7. To light the backdrop for a chroma key, you need (80) *Fresnel spotlights* (81) *ellipsoidal spotlights* (82) *floodlights*.

7	○ 80	○ 81	○ 82

8. The color temperature of a light can be raised by using (83) *an orange gel* (84) *a light-blue gel* (85) *an amber gel*.

8	○ 83	○ 84	○ 85

9. Having somebody stand in front of a brightly illuminated building will (86) *provide much needed back light* (87) *cause an undesirable silhouette effect* (88) *help separate the person from the background*.

9	○ 86	○ 87	○ 88

10. When shooting an ENG interview in bright sunlight, the most convenient fill light is (89) *an HMI spot* (90) *a quartz scoop* (91) *a reflector*.

10	○ 89	○ 90	○ 91

11. The standard color temperature for outdoor light in video is (92) *5,600K* (93) *3,600K* (94) *3,200K*.

11	○ 92	○ 93	○ 94

12. These lights fulfill similar functions: (95) *key and fill* (96) *back light and kicker* (97) *background light and kicker*.

12	○ 95	○ 96	○ 97

13. To make a model's hair look especially glamorous, you need a high-intensity (98) *key light* (99) *back light* (100) *background light*.

13	○ 98	○ 99	○ 100

14. The usual power rating per circuit of ordinary household wall outlets is (101) *15 amps* (102) *50 amps* (103) *150 amps*.

14	○ 101	○ 102	○ 103

15. To achieve fast falloff, you need to use primarily (104) *spotlights* (105) *floodlights* (106) *fluorescent lights*.

15	○ 104	○ 105	○ 106

16. To achieve a sharp shadow of a person cast onto a staircase wall, you need a (107) *focused Fresnel spot* (108) *Chinese lantern* (109) *softlight*.

16	○ 107	○ 108	○ 109

PAGE TOTAL [ ]

SECTION TOTAL [ ]

© 2012 Wadsworth, Cengage Learning

REVIEW QUIZ

*Mark the following statements as true or false by filling in the bubbles in the **T** (for true) or*
***F** (for false) column.*

		T	F
1.	The background light must strike the background from the same side as the key light.	1 ○ 110	○ 111
2.	Low-key lighting is best achieved with low-hanging softlights.	2 ○ 112	○ 113
3.	The photographic lighting principle, or triangle lighting, uses a key light, a kicker light, and a back light.	3 ○ 114	○ 115
4.	In multiple-function lighting, the key light can act as a back light, and the side light as key, depending on the position of the camera relative to the subject.	4 ○ 116	○ 117
5.	Back lights and background lights fulfill similar functions.	5 ○ 118	○ 119
6.	The less fill light, the slower the falloff.	6 ○ 120	○ 121
7.	An LED panel simulates more a spotlight than a floodlight.	7 ○ 122	○ 123
8.	Color temperature measures the relative reddishness and bluishness of white light.	8 ○ 124	○ 125
9.	All cameo lighting is highly directional.	9 ○ 126	○ 127
10.	In most cases, a reflector can substitute for a fill light.	10 ○ 128	○ 129
11.	Low-key lighting means that the lighting is soft and even, with extremely slow falloff.	11 ○ 130	○ 131
12.	Cast shadows can suggest a specific locale.	12 ○ 132	○ 133
13.	Plugging portable lights into different wall outlets means that they are automatically on different power circuits.	13 ○ 134	○ 135
14.	Two side lights can function similarly to a key and a fill.	14 ○ 136	○ 137
15.	High-key lighting means that the key light strikes the subject from above eye level.	15 ○ 138	○ 139

SECTION
TOTAL [   ]

© 2012 Wadsworth, Cengage Learning

PROBLEM-SOLVING APPLICATIONS

1. You are asked to do the lighting for a shampoo commercial. The director wants you to make the model's blond hair look especially brilliant and glamorous. Which of the three instruments of the lighting triangle needs special attention to achieve the desired result?

2. The show is a brief address by the CEO. Prepare a light plot for the floor plan shown at right. Sketch the type and the locations of the instruments used, as well as the general direction of the light beams.

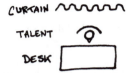

3. You (the camera operator) and a field reporter are sent by the assignment editor to the Plaza Hotel to interview a famous soprano in her room. The field reporter will remain off-camera during the entire interview. The lighting in the hotel room is inadequate, so you need additional lighting. Besides the camera light, you have only one Omni light at your disposal. Where would you place the Omni light? Why?

4. You are the LD for an indoor springtime fashion show. The studio audience is seated along both sides of the runway. The novice director suggests low-key lighting to give the show some extra sparkle. Do you agree with the director's suggestion? If so, why? If not, why not? What are your recommendations?

5. You are the LD for a dance number that plays in front of a light-gray cyc. The dancers wear off-white leotards. The choreographer wants them to appear first in cameo as illuminated figures against a dark blue background and then, in one continuous take, as black silhouettes moving against a bright red background. Can you fulfill the choreographer's request? If so, how? If not, why not?

6. You will be shooting an interview with the CEO of a large software company. Her office has a large window without any curtains. How would you light this interview while taking advantage of the daylight coming through the window? List specific lights, their locations, and all necessary support equipment.

7. You are covering the dedication of a new library. It is a cloudless, sunny day with the sun reflecting off the brilliant white building. The dedication is planned to happen right in front of the building. What are your concerns regarding lighting? What would you suggest to minimize some of the problems?

8. You are to light a two-anchor news set in which the two co-anchors (a dark-haired man and a blond woman) sit side-by-side. The man is worried about his wrinkles, especially because his co-anchor has perfectly smooth skin. What lighting would you suggest? Draw a rough light plot that indicates the type and the approximate locations of the instruments used.

© 2012 Wadsworth, Cengage Learning

13 Video-recording and Storage Systems

REVIEW OF KEY TERMS

Match each term with its appropriate definition by filling in the corresponding bubble.

1. **Y/color difference component system**
2. **composite system**
3. **field log**
4. **control track**
5. **time base corrector**
6. **JPEG**
7. **tapeless video recorder**
8. **Y/C component system**
9. **codec**
10. **ESS system**
11. **memory card**
12. **compression**
13. **MPEG-2**
14. **framestore synchronizer**

A. All digital video recorders that record or store information on a hard drive or read/write optical disc

A ○ ○ ○ ○ ○
   1 2 3 4 5
   ○ ○ ○ ○ ○
   6 7 8 9 10
   ○ ○ ○ ○
   11 12 13 14

B. A list of shots taken during the recording

B ○ ○ ○ ○ ○
   1 2 3 4 5
   ○ ○ ○ ○ ○
   6 7 8 9 10
   ○ ○ ○ ○
   11 12 13 14

C. A solid-state read/write digital storage media that has no moving parts

C ○ ○ ○ ○ ○
   1 2 3 4 5
   ○ ○ ○ ○ ○
   6 7 8 9 10
   ○ ○ ○ ○
   11 12 13 14

PAGE TOTAL [ ]

© 2012 Wadsworth, Cengage Learning

© 2012 Wadsworth, Cengage Learning

1. Y/color difference component system	5. time base corrector	10. ESS system	
2. composite system	6. JPEG	11. memory card	
3. field log	7. tapeless video recorder	12. compression	
4. control track	8. Y/C component system	13. MPEG-2	
	9. codec	14. framestore synchronizer	

D. Electronic accessory to a VTR that makes playbacks or transfers stable

D ○ ○ ○ ○ ○
  1 2 3 4 5
  ○ ○ ○ ○ ○
  6 7 8 9 10
  ○ ○ ○ ○
  11 12 13 14

E. A video signal in which luminance (Y), chrominance (C), and sync information are encoded into a single signal

E ○ ○ ○ ○ ○
  1 2 3 4 5
  ○ ○ ○ ○ ○
  6 7 8 9 10
  ○ ○ ○ ○
  11 12 13 14

F. A system in which the luminance (Y) and the R–Y and B–Y signals are kept separate throughout the video-recording process

F ○ ○ ○ ○ ○
  1 2 3 4 5
  ○ ○ ○ ○ ○
  6 7 8 9 10
  ○ ○ ○ ○
  11 12 13 14

G. A compression system generally used for digital television

G ○ ○ ○ ○ ○
  1 2 3 4 5
  ○ ○ ○ ○ ○
  6 7 8 9 10
  ○ ○ ○ ○
  11 12 13 14

H. Image stabilization and synchronization system that stores and reads out one complete video frame

H ○ ○ ○ ○ ○
  1 2 3 4 5
  ○ ○ ○ ○ ○
  6 7 8 9 10
  ○ ○ ○ ○
  11 12 13 14

PAGE TOTAL [ ]

I. The track on a videotape that contains synchronization information

I	○ 1	○ 2	○ 3	○ 4	○ 5
	○ 6	○ 7	○ 8	○ 9	○ 10
	○ 11	○ 12	○ 13	○ 14	

J. Reducing the amount of digital data for recording or transmission

J	○ 1	○ 2	○ 3	○ 4	○ 5
	○ 6	○ 7	○ 8	○ 9	○ 10
	○ 11	○ 12	○ 13	○ 14	

K. A system in which the luminance (Y) and chrominance (C) signals are kept separate during the encoding and decoding processes but are recorded together

K	○ 1	○ 2	○ 3	○ 4	○ 5
	○ 6	○ 7	○ 8	○ 9	○ 10
	○ 11	○ 12	○ 13	○ 14	

L. A video compression method mostly for still pictures

L	○ 1	○ 2	○ 3	○ 4	○ 5
	○ 6	○ 7	○ 8	○ 9	○ 10
	○ 11	○ 12	○ 13	○ 14	

M. A specific compression standard

M	○ 1	○ 2	○ 3	○ 4	○ 5
	○ 6	○ 7	○ 8	○ 9	○ 10
	○ 11	○ 12	○ 13	○ 14	

N. An electronic device that can grab and digitally store a single frame from any video source

N	○ 1	○ 2	○ 3	○ 4	○ 5
	○ 6	○ 7	○ 8	○ 9	○ 10
	○ 11	○ 12	○ 13	○ 14	

PAGE TOTAL [ ]

SECTION TOTAL [ ]

© 2012 Wadsworth, Cengage Learning

REVIEW OF TAPE-BASED AND TAPELESS VIDEO RECORDING

Select the correct answers and fill in the bubbles with the corresponding numbers.

1. Digital recording systems are (15) *nonlinear* (16) *linear* (17) *linear or nonlinear*, depending on the recording system.

   1 ○ 15 ○ 16 ○ 17

2. In contrast to digital recordings, analog recordings (18) *experience quality loss* (19) *remain the same* (20) *lose only color hue* from one generation to the next.

   2 ○ 18 ○ 19 ○ 20

3. Digital video signals can be recorded (21) *only on a computer disk* (22) *only on videotape* (23) *on tape as well as disk.*

   3 ○ 21 ○ 22 ○ 23

4. The NTSC signal is based on a (24) *Y/C component* (25) *composite* (26) *Y/color difference component* signal.

   4 ○ 24 ○ 25 ○ 26

5. Disk-based recording systems are always (27) *linear only* (28) *nonlinear only* (29) *both linear and nonlinear.*

   5 ○ 27 ○ 28 ○ 29

6. All tapeless systems (30) *have no moving parts* (31) *can record digital information only* (32) *can record video only.*

   6 ○ 30 ○ 31 ○ 32

7. An ESS system stores individual frames in (33) *digital only* (34) *analog only* (35) *both digital and analog form.*

   7 ○ 33 ○ 34 ○ 35

8. The type of compression that looks for redundancies from one frame to the next is (36) *interframe* (37) *intraframe* (38) *lossless.*

   8 ○ 36 ○ 37 ○ 38

9. You can use a ¼-inch DV mini-cassette for recording (39) *standard digital signals only* (40) *HDTV only* (41) *standard and HDTV signals.*

   9 ○ 39 ○ 40 ○ 41

10. The control track is essential for (42) *videotape recordings only* (43) *memory card recordings only* (44) *both tape and memory card recordings.*

    10 ○ 42 ○ 43 ○ 44

11. An ESS system can store (45) *individual video frames only* (46) *short video clips only* (47) *both frames and clips.*

    11 ○ 45 ○ 46 ○ 47

12. The Y/C component signal separates the (48) *color and luminance signals* (49) *audio and video signals* (50) *yellow and cyan color signals.*

    12 ○ 48 ○ 49 ○ 50

13. The best color fidelity is achieved through a (51) *4:2:2* (52) *4:1:1* (53) *4:0:0* sampling ratio.

    13 ○ 51 ○ 52 ○ 53

PAGE TOTAL [   ]

© 2012 Wadsworth, Cengage Learning

14. The illustration below shows a (54) *Y/C component signal* (55) *Y/color difference component signal* (56) *composite signal.*

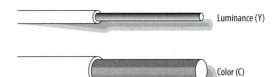

Luminance (Y)

Color (C)

| | 14 | ○ 54 | ○ 55 | ○ 56 |

15. Intraframe compression eliminates (57) *various frames* (58) *temporal redundancy in each frame* (59) *spatial redundancy in each frame.*

| | 15 | ○ 57 | ○ 58 | ○ 59 |

16. The digital recording system with no moving parts uses (60) *optical discs* (61) *hard drives* (62) *memory cards.*

| | 16 | ○ 60 | ○ 61 | ○ 62 |

17. One of the functions that distinguishes a server from a standard large-capacity hard drive is that the server can (63) *record large amounts of digital data* (64) *supply different material to various clients simultaneously* (65) *allow random access of clips.*

| | 17 | ○ 63 | ○ 64 | ○ 65 |

PAGE TOTAL

SECTION TOTAL

© 2012 Wadsworth, Cengage Learning

REVIEW OF HOW VIDEO RECORDING IS DONE

Select the correct answers and fill in the bubbles with the corresponding numbers.

1. Because color bars help the video-record operator match the technical aspects of the playback VR and the playback monitor, you should record them (66) *at the beginning of the video recording* (67) *right after the video leader* (68) *at the end of the video recording* for at least (69) *10 seconds* (70) *30 seconds* (71) *5 minutes.* **(Fill in two bubbles.)**

2. The field log is normally kept by the (72) *VR operator* (73) *TD* (74) *VO.*

3. To protect a cassette recording from being accidentally erased, the cassette tab (75) *must be in place or in the closed position* (76) *must be removed or in the open position* (77) *cannot prevent erasure.*

4. Nonlinear editing requires the transfer to the computer hard drive (78) *of only analog source media* (79) *of both analog and digital source media* (80) *of only digital source media.*

5. The clapboard aids in (81) *starting the countdown* (82) *synchronizing audio and video* (83) *marking the first video frame.*

6. Two essential items on a slate or clapboard are (84) *producer and date* (85) *title and take number* (86) *title and executive producer.*

7. When using a tapeless recording media, locating certain takes for recording checks is (87) *quicker than* (88) *slower than* (89) *about the same as* using videotape.

8. When beginning a recording, (90) *servers* (91) *memory cards* (92) *videotape recorders* need to reach operating speed to avoid video breakup.

9. Leader numbers are especially helpful for accurate cueing of (93) *servers* (94) *memory cards* (95) *videotape.*

10. You cannot import clips in a nonlinear editing system if it does not recognize the (96) *name* (97) *length* (98) *codec* of the clip.

11. The video leader (99) *should* (100) *should not* contain a 0 VU audio tone and (101) *should* (102) *should not* include the first frame of the recording. **(Fill in two bubbles.)**

1	○ 66	○ 67	○ 68
	○ 69	○ 70	○ 71
2	○ 72	○ 73	○ 74
3	○ 75	○ 76	○ 77
4	○ 78	○ 79	○ 80
5	○ 81	○ 82	○ 83
6	○ 84	○ 85	○ 86
7	○ 87	○ 88	○ 89
8	○ 90	○ 91	○ 92
9	○ 93	○ 94	○ 95
10	○ 96	○ 97	○ 98
11	○ 99	○ 100	
	○ 101	○ 102	

SECTION TOTAL

© 2012 Wadsworth, Cengage Learning

REVIEW QUIZ

*Mark the following statements as true or false by filling in the bubbles in the **T** (for true) or **F** (for false) column.*

		T	F
1.	The advantage of using a memory card for recording is that it can store more information than videotape.	1 ○ 103	○ 104
2.	You can use the SMPTE time code to mark frames of analog as well as digital recordings.	2 ○ 105	○ 106
3.	In a Y/color difference component system, the Y and R–Y/B–Y signals are kept separate throughout the entire recording process.	3 ○ 107	○ 108
4.	If they are lossy, all codecs are the same.	4 ○ 109	○ 110
5.	You can use videotape to record both analog and digital signals.	5 ○ 111	○ 112
6.	You can use a hard disk to record both analog and digital signals.	6 ○ 113	○ 114
7.	When dubbing videotapes, analog systems produce much more noise in subsequent generations than do digital ones.	7 ○ 115	○ 116
8.	A control track pulse marks each video frame.	8 ○ 117	○ 118
9.	The Y/C component system means that the color yellow has been added to the color signals.	9 ○ 119	○ 120
10.	You should use prerecorded color bars for the video leader.	10 ○ 121	○ 122
11.	A codec signifies a specific digital compression standard.	11 ○ 123	○ 124
12.	When a camera feeds a switcher in addition to its own VR, it is no longer an iso camera.	12 ○ 125	○ 126
13.	All tapeless storage systems allow random access.	13 ○ 127	○ 128
14.	MPEG-2 is an intraframe compression technique.	14 ○ 129	○ 130
15.	When digital information is stored on videotape, it allows random access.	15 ○ 131	○ 132
16.	A framestore synchronizer and a TBC fulfill similar functions.	16 ○ 133	○ 134
17.	All videotapes provide at least two audio tracks.	17 ○ 135	○ 136
18.	A 4:1:1 sampling ratio means that the color luminance signal is sampled four times as often as each color signal.	18 ○ 137	○ 138

SECTION TOTAL [   ]

© 2012 Wadsworth, Cengage Learning

PROBLEM-SOLVING APPLICATIONS

1. Before purchasing a new camcorder, why should you inquire about the codec it uses for recording?

2. You are asked to produce a brief instructional video on diagnosing specific skin rashes. The physician in charge insists that you use recording equipment that has a 4:2:2 sampling standard. Why is she so insistent about the sampling?

3. Because the extreme conditions under which the digital movie will be shot necessitate extensive audio postproduction and ADR, the editor insists on equipment that uses intraframe rather than interframe compression. Why do you think the editor specifies the compression system?

4. The department head asks you to defend the switch to a totally tapeless operation. What are your major arguments?

5. The novice digital cinema director tells you not to bother with videotape because it loses quality each time you dub it to another storage media. What is your reply?

6. How do intraframe and interframe compression relate to spatial and temporal redundancy?

© 2012 Wadsworth, Cengage Learning

Switching, or Instantaneous Editing

REVIEW OF KEY TERMS

Match each term with its appropriate definition by filling in the corresponding bubble.

1. delegation controls
2. program bus
3. key bus
4. fader bar
5. preview/preset bus

6. downstream keyer
7. switching
8. genlock
9. M/E bus
10. chroma key

11. auto-transition
12. DVE
13. super
14. wipe
15. matte key

A. Control that allows a title to be keyed over the line-out image as it leaves the switcher

A
○1 ○2 ○3 ○4 ○5
○6 ○7 ○8 ○9 ○10
○11 ○12 ○13 ○14 ○15

B. A button that triggers the function of a fader bar

B
○1 ○2 ○3 ○4 ○5
○6 ○7 ○8 ○9 ○10
○11 ○12 ○13 ○14 ○15

C. Rows of buttons used to select the upcoming video and route it to the preview monitor

C
○1 ○2 ○3 ○4 ○5
○6 ○7 ○8 ○9 ○10
○11 ○12 ○13 ○14 ○15

P A G E
T O T A L   [   ]

© 2012 Wadsworth, Cengage Learning

1. delegation controls	6. downstream keyer	11. auto-transition
2. program bus	7. switching	12. DVE
3. key bus	8. genlock	13. super
4. fader bar	9. M/E bus	14. wipe
5. preview/preset bus	10. chroma key	15. matte key

D. A change from one video source to the next

D ① ② ③ ④ ⑤ (1 2 3 4 5)
   ⑥ ⑦ ⑧ ⑨ ⑩ (6 7 8 9 10)
   ⑪ ⑫ ⑬ ⑭ ⑮ (11 12 13 14 15)

E. A row of buttons that can serve a mix or an effects function

E ① ② ③ ④ ⑤ (1 2 3 4 5)
   ⑥ ⑦ ⑧ ⑨ ⑩ (6 7 8 9 10)
   ⑪ ⑫ ⑬ ⑭ ⑮ (11 12 13 14 15)

F. Electronically cut-in title whose letters are filled with shades of gray or a specific color

F ① ② ③ ④ ⑤ (1 2 3 4 5)
   ⑥ ⑦ ⑧ ⑨ ⑩ (6 7 8 9 10)
   ⑪ ⑫ ⑬ ⑭ ⑮ (11 12 13 14 15)

G. A double exposure of two images

G ① ② ③ ④ ⑤ (1 2 3 4 5)
   ⑥ ⑦ ⑧ ⑨ ⑩ (6 7 8 9 10)
   ⑪ ⑫ ⑬ ⑭ ⑮ (11 12 13 14 15)

H. Controls on a switcher that assign specific functions to a bus

H ① ② ③ ④ ⑤ (1 2 3 4 5)
   ⑥ ⑦ ⑧ ⑨ ⑩ (6 7 8 9 10)
   ⑪ ⑫ ⑬ ⑭ ⑮ (11 12 13 14 15)

PAGE TOTAL [   ]

© 2012 Wadsworth, Cengage Learning

I. A lever on the switcher that activates preset functions such as dissolves, fades, and wipes of varying speeds

I
1 ○ 2 ○ 3 ○ 4 ○ 5 ○
6 ○ 7 ○ 8 ○ 9 ○ 10 ○
11 ○ 12 ○ 13 ○ 14 ○ 15 ○

J. Effect that uses color (usually blue or green) for the backdrop, which is replaced by the background image

J
1 ○ 2 ○ 3 ○ 4 ○ 5 ○
6 ○ 7 ○ 8 ○ 9 ○ 10 ○
11 ○ 12 ○ 13 ○ 14 ○ 15 ○

K. A bus used to select the video source to be inserted into a background image

K
1 ○ 2 ○ 3 ○ 4 ○ 5 ○
6 ○ 7 ○ 8 ○ 9 ○ 10 ○
11 ○ 12 ○ 13 ○ 14 ○ 15 ○

L. Transition in which the new image is revealed in a pattern or shape

L
1 ○ 2 ○ 3 ○ 4 ○ 5 ○
6 ○ 7 ○ 8 ○ 9 ○ 10 ○
11 ○ 12 ○ 13 ○ 14 ○ 15 ○

M. The bus on a switcher whose inputs are directly switched to the line-out

M
1 ○ 2 ○ 3 ○ 4 ○ 5 ○
6 ○ 7 ○ 8 ○ 9 ○ 10 ○
11 ○ 12 ○ 13 ○ 14 ○ 15 ○

N. Visual effects generated by computer or the software in the switcher

N
1 ○ 2 ○ 3 ○ 4 ○ 5 ○
6 ○ 7 ○ 8 ○ 9 ○ 10 ○
11 ○ 12 ○ 13 ○ 14 ○ 15 ○

P A G E
T O T A L [   ]

© 2012 Wadsworth, Cengage Learning

W-161

Select the correct answers and fill in the bubbles with the corresponding numbers.

2. To select the functions of a specific bus or buses, you need to activate the (24) *joystick* (25) *wipe mode selectors* (26) *delegation controls.*

3. The program bus will direct the selected video source to the (27) *preview monitor* (28) *mix bus* (29) *line-out.*

4. To dissolve from C3 (camera 3) to VR (with the auto-transition in the *off* position), you (30) *press the VR button on the preview bus; then press the cut button* (31) *press the VR button on the preview bus; then move the fader bar to the opposite position* (32) *press the VR button on the key bus; then move the fader bar to the opposite position.*

5. To have C3 appear on the preview monitor before switching to it from C1, you need to (33) *press C3 on the preview bus* (34) *press C3 on the preview bus; then press the key button* (35) *press C3 on the program bus; then move the fader bar to the opposite position.*

6. To switch from C1 to C3 by pressing only one button, you need to press the (36) *C3 button on the preview bus* (37) *C3 button on the key bus* (38) *C3 button on the program bus.* **(This assumes that the appropriate buses have already been delegated a mix/effects function.)**

7. Assuming that the final C.G. credits are keyed with the DSK, you can go to black by (39) *pressing the black button on the program bus* (40) *pressing the black button on the key bus* (41) *pressing the black button in the downstream keyer section.*

2	◯ 24	◯ 25	◯ 26
3	◯ 27	◯ 28	◯ 29
4	◯ 30	◯ 31	◯ 32
5	◯ 33	◯ 34	◯ 35
6	◯ 36	◯ 37	◯ 38
7	◯ 39	◯ 40	◯ 41

P A G E
T O T A L

PART III *PRODUCTION*

© 2012 Wadsworth, Cengage Learning

8. Identify the proper preview and line monitor images you would expect to see from the switcher output by filling in the corresponding bubble. The highlighted buttons on the following switcher have already been pressed. C1 is focused on the host, C2 on the dancers (see the monitor images below).

PHOTOS: EDWARD AIONA

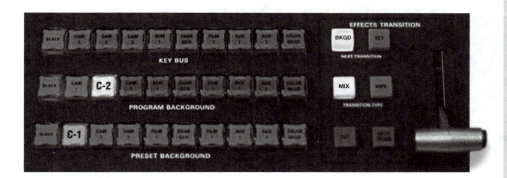

8 ○ 42   ○ 43   ○ 44

42

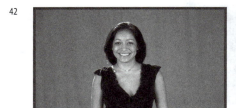

Preview

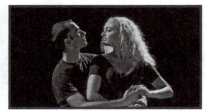

Line

43

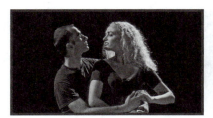

Preview

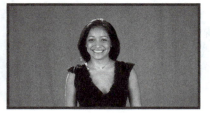

Line

44

Preview

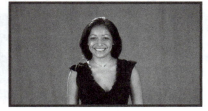

Line

PAGE
TOTAL [   ]

© 2012 Wadsworth, Cengage Learning

9. Identify the proper preview and line monitor images you would expect to see from the switcher output and fill in the corresponding bubble.

PHOTOS: EDWARD AIONA

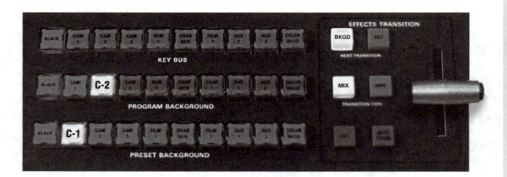

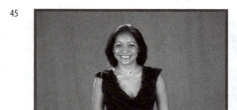

45

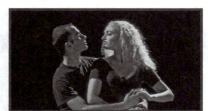

Preview

Line

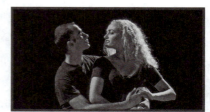

46

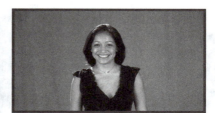

Preview

Line

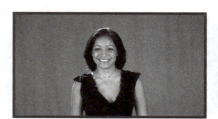

47

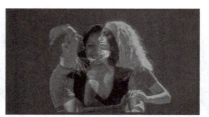

Preview

Line

9 ◯ 45 ◯ 46 ◯ 47

P A G E
T O T A L

© 2012 Wadsworth, Cengage Learning

10. Identify the proper preview and line monitor images you would expect to see from the switcher output at the end of the previous dissolve and fill in the corresponding bubble.

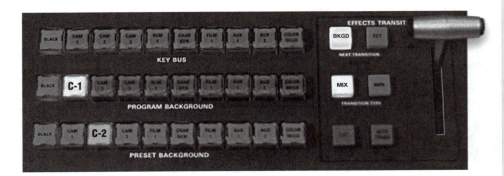

48

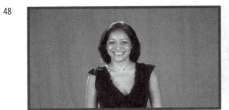

Preview

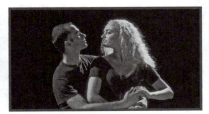

Line

49

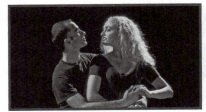

Preview

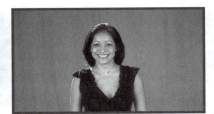

Line

50

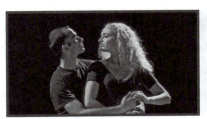

Preview

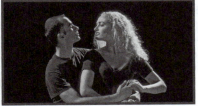

Line

PHOTOS: EDWARD AIONA

© 2012 Wadsworth, Cengage Learning

PAGE TOTAL [ ]

SECTION TOTAL [ ]

REVIEW OF ELECTRONIC EFFECTS AND SWITCHER FUNCTIONS

1. Fill in the bubbles whose numbers correspond with the appropriate electronic effects illustrated in the following figures.

51
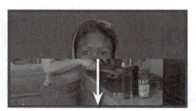

52
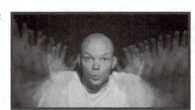

53
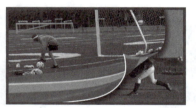

54
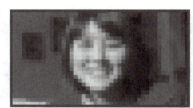

55
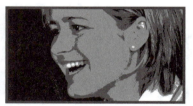

56
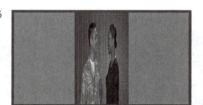

57
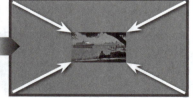

58
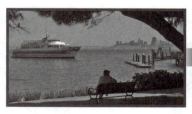

59
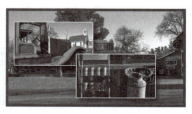

PHOTOS: EDWARD AIONA

© 2012 Wadsworth, Cengage Learning

a. vertical stretching

1a ○ ○ ○ ○ ○
    51 52 53 54 55
    ○ ○ ○ ○
    56 57 58 59

b. echo effect

1b ○ ○ ○ ○ ○
    51 52 53 54 55
    ○ ○ ○ ○
    56 57 58 59

c. horizontal wipe

1c ○ ○ ○ ○ ○
    51 52 53 54 55
    ○ ○ ○ ○
    56 57 58 59

d. peel effect

1d ○ ○ ○ ○ ○
    51 52 53 54 55
    ○ ○ ○ ○
    56 57 58 59

e. posterization

1e ○ ○ ○ ○ ○
    51 52 53 54 55
    ○ ○ ○ ○
    56 57 58 59

f. shrinking

1f ○ ○ ○ ○ ○
    51 52 53 54 55
    ○ ○ ○ ○
    56 57 58 59

g. vertical wipe

1g ○ ○ ○ ○ ○
    51 52 53 54 55
    ○ ○ ○ ○
    56 57 58 59

h. multiple frames

1h ○ ○ ○ ○ ○
    51 52 53 54 55
    ○ ○ ○ ○
    56 57 58 59

i. mosaic

1i ○ ○ ○ ○ ○
    51 52 53 54 55
    ○ ○ ○ ○
    56 57 58 59

P A G E
T O T A L [ ]

© 2012 Wadsworth, Cengage Learning

2. Fill in the bubbles whose numbers correspond with the button you would have to press on the pattern selector to create the various effects illustrated in the following figures.

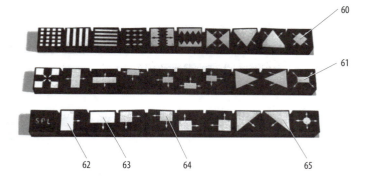

a.

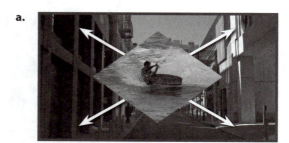

b.

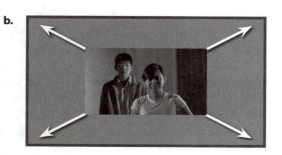

2a ◯ 60   ◯ 61   ◯ 62
    ◯ 63   ◯ 64   ◯ 65

2b ◯ 60   ◯ 61   ◯ 62
    ◯ 63   ◯ 64   ◯ 65

PHOTOS: EDWARD AIONA

PAGE TOTAL

© 2012 Wadsworth, Cengage Learning

c.

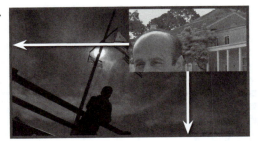

PHOTOS: EDWARD AIONA

d.

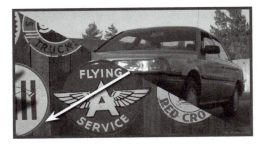

e.

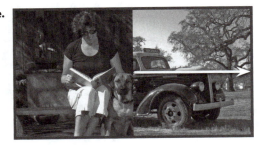

f.

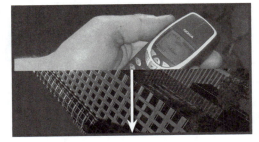

2c	60 ○	61 ○	62 ○
	63 ○	64 ○	65 ○

2d	60 ○	61 ○	62 ○
	63 ○	64 ○	65 ○

2e	60 ○	61 ○	62 ○
	63 ○	64 ○	65 ○

2f	60 ○	61 ○	62 ○
	63 ○	64 ○	65 ○

PAGE
TOTAL [ ]

© 2012 Wadsworth, Cengage Learning

3. Fill in the bubbles whose numbers correspond with the appropriate key effects shown in the following figures.

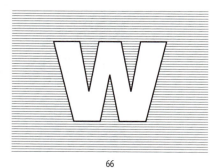

66

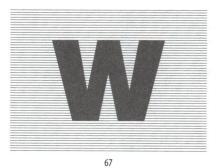

67

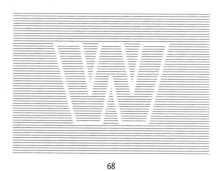

68

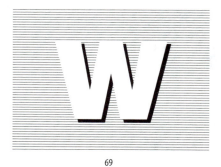

69

a. edge mode

b. outline mode

c. drop-shadow mode

d. matte key

3a	◯ 66	◯ 67	◯ 68	◯ 69
3b	◯ 66	◯ 67	◯ 68	◯ 69
3c	◯ 66	◯ 67	◯ 68	◯ 69
3d	◯ 66	◯ 67	◯ 68	◯ 69

PAGE TOTAL

© 2012 Wadsworth, Cengage Learning

Select the correct answers and fill in the bubbles with the corresponding numbers.

4. The two most frequently used backdrop colors for studio chroma-key effects are (70) *green and blue* (71) *blue and red* (72) *yellow and blue.*

5. A peel effect (73) *reveals the picture underneath* (74) *strips the picture of detail* (75) *covers the current picture.*

6. To create echo, stretching, and compression effects, you need (76) *DVE* (77) *a CCU* (78) *a TBC.*

7. A secondary frame (screen within a screen) (79) *must have a 4 × 3 horizontal aspect ratio* (80) *must have a 16 × 9 HDTV aspect ratio* (81) *can have a vertical aspect ratio.*

8. Shrinking effects differ from box wipes because (82) *they maintain the total picture and aspect ratio during the reduction* (83) *the reduction can get smaller than a box wipe* (84) *they need a blue background.*

9. When the talent insists on wearing blue for a standard chroma-key effect, the backdrop color must be (85) *blue* (86) *green* (87) *yellow.*

10. During posterization (88) *the brightness values are reduced* (89) *the saturation is reversed* (90) *all brightness values are reversed.*

4	○ 70	○ 71	○ 72
5	○ 73	○ 74	○ 75
6	○ 76	○ 77	○ 78
7	○ 79	○ 80	○ 81
8	○ 82	○ 83	○ 84
9	○ 85	○ 86	○ 87
10	○ 88	○ 89	○ 90

PAGE TOTAL _____

SECTION TOTAL _____

© 2012 Wadsworth, Cengage Learning

Design

REVIEW OF KEY TERMS

Match each term with its appropriate definition by filling in the corresponding bubble.

1. **color compatibility**
2. **windowbox**
3. **props**
4. **floor plan pattern**

5. **scanning area**
6. **essential area**
7. **C.G.**
8. **floor plan**

9. **pillarbox**
10. **flat**
11. **letterbox**
12. **graphics generator**

A. The picture area usually seen on the camera viewfinder and the preview monitor

A
1 2 3 4
5 6 7 8
9 10 11 12

B. Furniture and other objects used for set decorations or by actors or performers

B
1 2 3 4
5 6 7 8
9 10 11 12

C. Colors with enough brightness contrast for good monochrome reproduction

C
1 2 3 4
5 6 7 8
9 10 11 12

P A G E
T O T A L

© 2012 Wadsworth, Cengage Learning

1.	color compatibility	5.	scanning area	9.	pillarbox
2.	windowbox	6.	essential area	10.	flat
3.	props	7.	C.G.	11.	letterbox
4.	floor plan pattern	8.	floor plan	12.	graphics generator

D. Computer software that allows a designer to draw, color, animate, store, and retrieve images electronically

D ○ ○ ○ ○
   1 2 3 4
  ○ ○ ○ ○
   5 6 7 8
  ○ ○ ○ ○
   9 10 11 12

E. The section of the television picture, centered within the scanning area, that the home viewer sees

E ○ ○ ○ ○
   1 2 3 4
  ○ ○ ○ ○
   5 6 7 8
  ○ ○ ○ ○
   9 10 11 12

F. Fitting a 16×9 aspect ratio into a 4×3 screen without cropping or distortion

F ○ ○ ○ ○
   1 2 3 4
  ○ ○ ○ ○
   5 6 7 8
  ○ ○ ○ ○
   9 10 11 12

G. A plan of the studio floor with the grid but without a set design

G ○ ○ ○ ○
   1 2 3 4
  ○ ○ ○ ○
   5 6 7 8
  ○ ○ ○ ○
   9 10 11 12

H. A smaller frame positioned in the center of the TV screen.

H ○ ○ ○ ○
   1 2 3 4
  ○ ○ ○ ○
   5 6 7 8
  ○ ○ ○ ○
   9 10 11 12

PAGE TOTAL [ ]

© 2012 Wadsworth, Cengage Learning

I. A piece of standing scenery used as a background or to simulate a wall

I ○ ○ ○ ○
   1 2 3 4
   ○ ○ ○ ○
   5 6 7 8
   ○ ○ ○ ○
   9 10 11 12

J. A diagram of scenery and major set properties drawn on a grid

J ○ ○ ○ ○
   1 2 3 4
   ○ ○ ○ ○
   5 6 7 8
   ○ ○ ○ ○
   9 10 11 12

K. Fitting a 4 × 3 aspect ratio into a 16 × 9 screen without cropping or distortion

K ○ ○ ○ ○
   1 2 3 4
   ○ ○ ○ ○
   5 6 7 8
   ○ ○ ○ ○
   9 10 11 12

L. A dedicated computer that electronically produces letters, numbers, and simple graphic images for video display

L ○ ○ ○ ○
   1 2 3 4
   ○ ○ ○ ○
   5 6 7 8
   ○ ○ ○ ○
   9 10 11 12

PAGE TOTAL [ ]

SECTION TOTAL [ ]

© 2012 Wadsworth, Cengage Learning

REVIEW OF TELEVISION GRAPHICS

Select the correct answers and fill in the bubbles with the corresponding numbers.

1. On a grayscale *1* represents (13) *TV white* (14) *TV black* (15) *100 percent reflectance.*

2. Color compatibility refers to using colors that differ distinctly as to (16) *hue* (17) *saturation* (18) *brightness.*

3. Dead zones are (19) *uninteresting picture areas* (20) *the empty vertical bars when showing standard TV on HDTV* (21) *a sound problem in studio areas.*

4. The whiteboard writing shown in the photo below is (22) *appropriate* (23) *inappropriate* because it (24) *is within the scanning area* (25) *does not permit good CUs.* **(Fill in two bubbles.)**

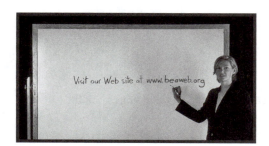

5. All lettering must be contained within the (26) *scanning area* (27) *screen area* (28) *essential area.*

6. The standard television aspect ratio is (29) *4 × 3* (30) *8 × 12* (31) *16 × 9.* For HDTV it is (32) *4 × 3* (33) *8 × 12* (34) *16 × 9.* **(Fill in two bubbles.)**

7. Normally, low-energy colors are used more for the (35) *foreground* (36) *middleground* (37) *background* in a scene.

8. To store a great many video frames for instant access, you need (38) *an ESS system* (39) *DVE* (40) *an SEG.*

9. The aesthetic energy of a color is principally determined by (41) *hue and brightness* (42) *the color itself* (43) *saturation and brightness.*

1	○ 13	○ 14	○ 15
2	○ 16	○ 17	○ 18
3	○ 19	○ 20	○ 21
4	○ 22	○ 23	
	○ 24	○ 25	
5	○ 26	○ 27	○ 28
6	○ 29	○ 30	○ 31
	○ 32	○ 33	○ 34
7	○ 35	○ 36	○ 37
8	○ 38	○ 39	○ 40
9	○ 41	○ 42	○ 43

PAGE TOTAL

PHOTO: EDWARD AIONA

© 2012 Wadsworth, Cengage Learning

10. Fill in the bubbles whose numbers correspond with the appropriate aspect ratio or frame adjustments in the figure.

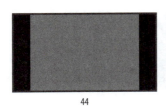 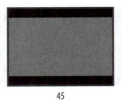 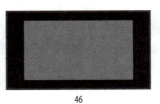

44   45   46

a. windowbox

b. letterbox

c. pillarbox

11. The vertically oriented diagram below is (47) *acceptable* (48) *not acceptable* for shooting with a studio camera because (49) *it is not in proper aspect ratio* (50) *the camera can tilt in a close-up.* (**Fill in two bubbles.**)

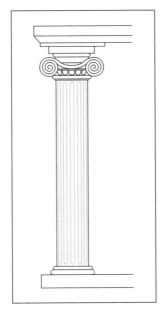

	44	45	46
10a	○	○	○
10b	○	○	○
10c	○	○	○

11 ○ 47   ○ 48
     ○ 49   ○ 50

P A G E
T O T A L ▢

© 2012 Wadsworth, Cengage Learning

W-181

12. The edge distortion as shown in the figure below is called (51) *aliasing* (52) *anti-aliasing* (53) *pixel distortion*.

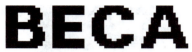

13. Fill in the bubbles whose numbers correspond with the appropriate title areas in the following figure.

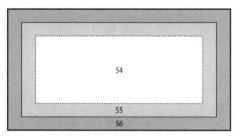

    a. total graphic screen area

    b. essential area

    c. scanning area

14. Fill in the bubbles whose numbers correspond with the type of digital distortion that results from adjusting one aspect ratio to fit another.

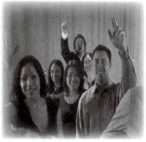 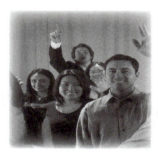

        57   58

    a. a 16 × 9 shot viewed full-screen on a 4 × 3 monitor

    b. a 4 × 3 shot viewed full-screen on a 16 × 9 monitor

12	○ 51	○ 52	○ 53
13a	○ 54	○ 55	○ 56
13b	○ 54	○ 55	○ 56
13c	○ 54	○ 55	○ 56
14a	○ 57	○ 58	
14b	○ 57	○ 58	

P A G E
T O T A L

PHOTOS: EDWARD AIONA

© 2012 Wadsworth, Cengage Learning

15. The following six figures show various television graphics displayed on well-adjusted preview monitors. These monitors show the entire scanning area. For each figure state whether you would (59) *accept* (60) *not accept* the television graphic because it has (61) *inappropriate style* (62) *enough contrast between figure and ground* (63) *scattered information* (64) *good grouping of words* (65) *letters that are too small* (66) *information that lies outside the essential area* (67) *letters that get lost in the busy background*. ***(Fill in the two bubbles that seem most appropriate for each graphic.)***

Nuclear Crisis

a.

Design by
Gary Palmatier

b.

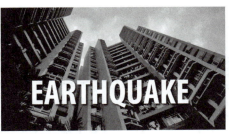

EARTHQUAKE

c.

Zoom control ring

Focus ring   Iris control ring

d.

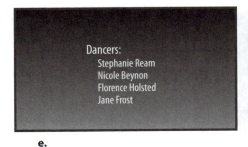

Dancers:
Stephanie Ream
Nicole Beynon
Florence Holsted
Jane Frost

e.

Crew

Susan Walters   Robaire Ream
Cathy Linberg   Karen Austin
        Deirdre Cavanaugh
Elizabeth von Radics
Ryan E. Vesely   Mike Mollett
    Ken Baird   Dory Schaeffer
    Stacey Purviance

f.

15a ○ 59   ○ 60
○ 61 ○ 62 ○ 63 ○ 64
○ 65 ○ 66 ○ 67

15b ○ 59   ○ 60
○ 61 ○ 62 ○ 63 ○ 64
○ 65 ○ 66 ○ 67

15c ○ 59   ○ 60
○ 61 ○ 62 ○ 63 ○ 64
○ 65 ○ 66 ○ 67

15d ○ 59   ○ 60
○ 61 ○ 62 ○ 63 ○ 64
○ 65 ○ 66 ○ 67

15e ○ 59   ○ 60
○ 61 ○ 62 ○ 63 ○ 64
○ 65 ○ 66 ○ 67

15f ○ 59   ○ 60
○ 61 ○ 62 ○ 63 ○ 64
○ 65 ○ 66 ○ 67

PAGE TOTAL [ ]

SECTION TOTAL [ ]

PHOTO: HERBERT ZETTL

© 2012 Wadsworth, Cengage Learning

REVIEW OF SCENERY AND SCENIC DESIGN

1. For the simple sets shown below, select the floor plan shown on the facing page that most closely corresponds and fill in the appropriate bubbles. *(Assume that the camera shoots straight-on. Note that there are floor plans that do not match any of the set photos. The floor plans are not to scale.)*

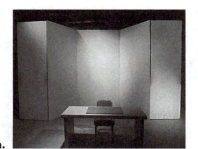

a.

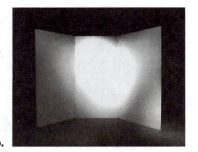

b.

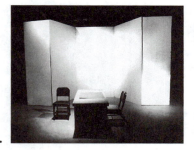

c.

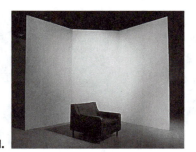

d.

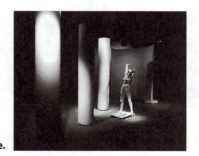

e.

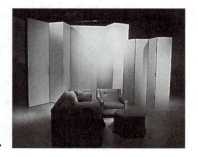

f.

1a ○ ○ ○ ○ ○
68 69 70 71 72
○ ○ ○ ○
73 74 75 76

1b ○ ○ ○ ○ ○
68 69 70 71 72
○ ○ ○ ○
73 74 75 76

1c ○ ○ ○ ○ ○
68 69 70 71 72
○ ○ ○ ○
73 74 75 76

1d ○ ○ ○ ○ ○
68 69 70 71 72
○ ○ ○ ○
73 74 75 76

1e ○ ○ ○ ○ ○
68 69 70 71 72
○ ○ ○ ○
73 74 75 76

1f ○ ○ ○ ○ ○
68 69 70 71 72
○ ○ ○ ○
73 74 75 76

P A G E
T O T A L

PHOTOS: HERBERT ZETTL

© 2012 Wadsworth, Cengage Learning

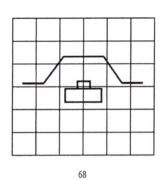

68

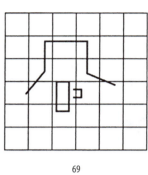

69

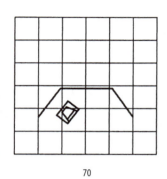

70

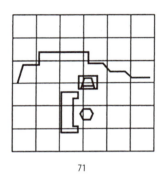

71

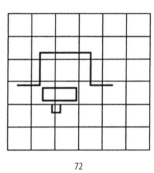

72

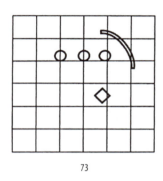

73

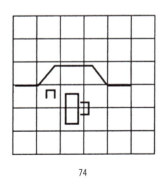

74

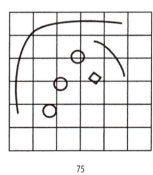

75

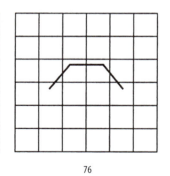

76

© 2012 Wadsworth, Cengage Learning

CHAPTER 15 *DESIGN*

2. Fill in the bubbles whose numbers correspond with the numbers identifying the various set pieces shown below.

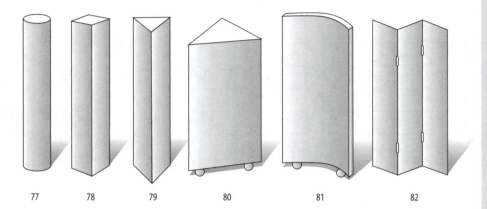

77   78   79   80   81   82

a. sweep

b. round pillar

c. periaktos

d. screen

e. square pillar

f. pylon

2a ○ 77	○ 78	○ 79
○ 80	○ 81	○ 82
2b ○ 77	○ 78	○ 79
○ 80	○ 81	○ 82
2c ○ 77	○ 78	○ 79
○ 80	○ 81	○ 82
2d ○ 77	○ 78	○ 79
○ 80	○ 81	○ 82
2e ○ 77	○ 78	○ 79
○ 80	○ 81	○ 82
2f ○ 77	○ 78	○ 79
○ 80	○ 81	○ 82

P A G E
T O T A L

© 2012 Wadsworth, Cengage Learning

Select the correct answers and fill in the bubbles with the corresponding numbers.

3. The usual height for standard set units is (83) *7 feet* (84) *10 feet* (85) *14 feet*. For studios with low ceilings, it is (86) *6 feet* (87) *8 feet* (88) *12 feet*. **(Fill in two bubbles.)**

3 ○ ○ ○
   83   84   85
   ○ ○ ○
   86   87   88

4. To elevate scenery, properties, or action areas, we use (89) *periaktoi* (90) *platforms* (91) *pylons*.

4 ○ ○ ○
   89   90   91

5. Pictures and draperies are (92) *set dressings* (93) *set decorations* (94) *hand props*.

5 ○ ○ ○
   92   93   94

6. The continuous piece of canvas or muslin along two, three, or even all four studio walls to form a uniform background is referred to as (95) *a drop* (96) *canvas backing* (97) *a cyclorama*.

6 ○ ○ ○
   95   96   97

7. The standard backgrounds to simulate interior and exterior walls are called (98) *cycs* (99) *flats* (100) *drops*.

7 ○ ○ ○
   98   99   100

PAGE TOTAL [ ]

SECTION TOTAL [ ]

© 2012 Wadsworth, Cengage Learning

*Mark the following statements as true or false by filling in the bubbles in the **T** (for true) or*
***F** (for false) column.*

		T	F
1.	A good floor plan will aid the LD in the lighting design.	**1** ○ 101	○ 102
2.	The energy of a color is determined primarily by hue.	**2** ○ 103	○ 104
3.	A periaktos looks like a large pylon.	**3** ○ 105	○ 106
4.	A black drape makes an ideal chroma-key backdrop.	**4** ○ 107	○ 108
5.	There is an inevitable picture loss when wide-screen movies are shown in their true aspect ratio on a traditional (4 x 3) television screen.	**5** ○ 109	○ 110
6.	Distinctly different hues (such as red and green) guarantee good brightness contrast.	**6** ○ 111	○ 112
7.	For normal screen titles, all written information must extend beyond the scanning area.	**7** ○ 113	○ 114
8.	A floor plan must show the location of flats but can omit the set properties.	**8** ○ 115	○ 116
9.	The scanning area is contained within the essential area.	**9** ○ 117	○ 118
10.	Hardwall scenery is preferred for permanent sets.	**10** ○ 119	○ 120
11.	Pillarboxing is used to fit a 4 × 3 aspect ratio into a 16 × 9 screen without distortion.	**11** ○ 121	○ 122
12.	Screen clutter can be avoided by grouping related information in specific screen areas.	**12** ○ 123	○ 124
13.	So long as there are distinct colors, brightness differences are relatively unimportant in digital cinema.	**13** ○ 125	○ 126
14.	Writing across a whiteboard from edge to edge facilitates CUs of the entire text.	**14** ○ 127	○ 128
15.	Bold lettering is especially important for mobile media displays.	**15** ○ 129	○ 130
16.	Digitally stretching a 4 × 3 scene to fill a 16 × 9 screen will make the people in it appear fat.	**16** ○ 131	○ 132

SECTION
TOTAL

© 2012 Wadsworth, Cengage Learning

PROBLEM-SOLVING APPLICATIONS

1. You are asked to direct a variety of shows and evaluate the location sketch or floor plans (see **a** through **c**). Please be specific as to the potential problems in scale (sets and props), camera accessibility and acceptable shots, lighting, and talent traffic.

   a. Here is a floor plan for a two-camera live-recorded production of a panel discussion by six prominent businesspeople and a moderator.

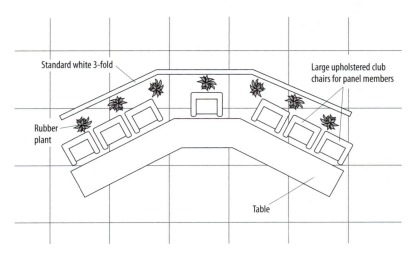

   b. This floor plan is for a two-camera live interview set for a morning show.

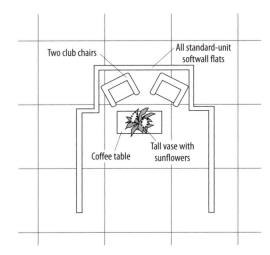

c. This location sketch shows the office of the CEO, who would like to make her monthly 4 p.m. live-satellite TV report from behind her desk.

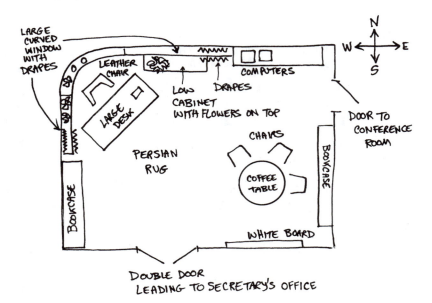

2. Draw a floor plan for a weekly interview show dealing with the art and media scene in your city. The host will interview guests from stage, screen, and radio. Include a detailed prop list. (Use one of the floor plan patterns provided at the back of this book.)

3. Draw a floor plan for a morning news set. The anchors are a woman and a man, and the news content is geared more toward local gossip than international politics. (Use one of the floor plan patterns provided at the back of this book.)

4. The general manager of your corporation would like you to use a highly detailed photo of the latest computer design as the background for the opening and closing titles. Can you accommodate the request and still make the titles optimally readable?

5. The art director proudly shows you the dancing Chinese-like lettering he has created with his titling software for the name identification of the new Chinese consul. Would you use such a title key? If so, why? If not, why not?

© 2012 Wadsworth, Cengage Learning

Television Talent

REVIEW OF KEY TERMS

Match each term with its appropriate definition by filling in the corresponding bubble.

1. performer	4. makeup	7. pan-stick
2. talent	5. blocking	8. teleprompter
3. actor	6. cue card	

A. Carefully worked-out position, movement, and actions by the talent

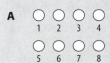

B. A person who appears on-camera in a nondramatic role

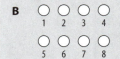

C. A person who appears on-camera in a dramatic role

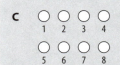

D. A large, hand-lettered card that contains on-air copy

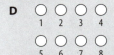

PAGE TOTAL [ ]

© 2012 Wadsworth, Cengage Learning

1. performer	4. makeup	7. pan-stick
2. talent	5. blocking	8. teleprompter
3. actor	6. cue card	

E. All people who regularly appear on television

E
○ ○ ○ ○
1 2 3 4
○ ○ ○ ○
5 6 7 8

F. Cosmetics used to enhance, correct, or change appearance.

F
○ ○ ○ ○
1 2 3 4
○ ○ ○ ○
5 6 7 8

G. Foundation makeup with a grease base

G
○ ○ ○ ○
1 2 3 4
○ ○ ○ ○
5 6 7 8

H. Also known as auto-cue

H
○ ○ ○ ○
1 2 3 4
○ ○ ○ ○
5 6 7 8

PAGE TOTAL [   ]

SECTION TOTAL [   ]

© 2012 Wadsworth, Cengage Learning

REVIEW OF PERFORMING TECHNIQUES

1. The following pictures show various *time* cues given to the talent by the floor manager. From the list below, select the specific cue illustrated and fill in the bubble with the corresponding number.

(9) 5 minutes left	(13) stretch	(16) standby
(10) 30 seconds left	(14) cut	(17) cue
(11) 15 seconds left	(15) wind up	(18) speed up
(12) on time		

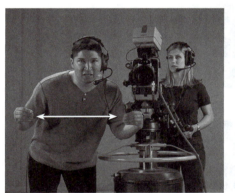

a.

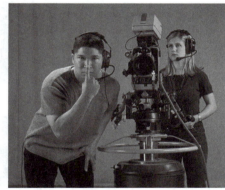

b.

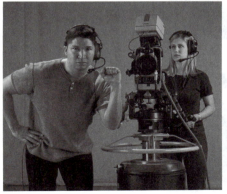

c.

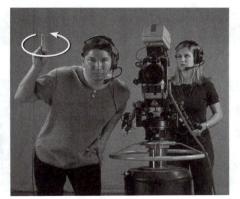

d.

1a ○ ○ ○ ○ ○
    9 10 11 12 13
    ○ ○ ○ ○ ○
   14 15 16 17 18

1b ○ ○ ○ ○ ○
    9 10 11 12 13
    ○ ○ ○ ○ ○
   14 15 16 17 18

1c ○ ○ ○ ○ ○
    9 10 11 12 13
    ○ ○ ○ ○ ○
   14 15 16 17 18

1d ○ ○ ○ ○ ○
    9 10 11 12 13
    ○ ○ ○ ○ ○
   14 15 16 17 18

PAGE TOTAL [ ]

PHOTOS: EDWARD AIONA

© 2012 Wadsworth, Cengage Learning

(19) keep talking	(22) walk	(25) tone down
(20) step back	(23) speak up	(26) closer
(21) OK	(24) closer to mic	

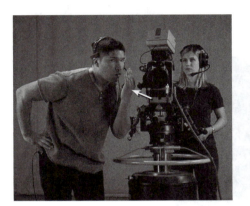

e.

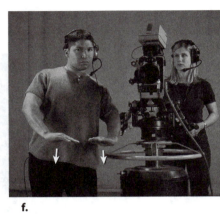

f.

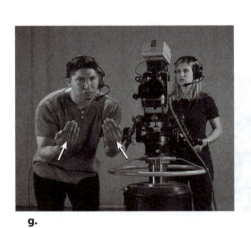

g.

h.

2e ◯ ◯ ◯ ◯
   19 20 21 22
  ◯ ◯ ◯ ◯
   23 24 25 26

2f ◯ ◯ ◯ ◯
   19 20 21 22
  ◯ ◯ ◯ ◯
   23 24 25 26

2g ◯ ◯ ◯ ◯
   19 20 21 22
  ◯ ◯ ◯ ◯
   23 24 25 26

2h ◯ ◯ ◯ ◯
   19 20 21 22
  ◯ ◯ ◯ ◯
   23 24 25 26

PAGE TOTAL

PHOTOS: EDWARD AIONA

© 2012 Wadsworth, Cengage Learning

Select the correct answers and fill in the bubbles with the corresponding numbers.

3. From the list below, select the microphone most appropriate for the various performance and acting tasks and fill in the bubbles with the corresponding numbers.

(27) lavalier   (30) fishpole mic   (33) wireless hand mic

(28) boom mic   (31) stand mic   (34) wireless lavalier

(29) hand mic   (32) desk mic

a. lead guitarist with a rock band, who also sings and talks to the audience from the stage

3a ○ ○ ○ ○
   27 28 29 30
   ○ ○ ○ ○
   31 32 33 34

b. two actors doing an outdoor scene

3b ○ ○ ○ ○
   27 28 29 30
   ○ ○ ○ ○
   31 32 33 34

c. singer who is also doing brief dance steps, accompanied by a large band

3c ○ ○ ○ ○
   27 28 29 30
   ○ ○ ○ ○
   31 32 33 34

d. interview with a celebrity at a busy airport gate

3d ○ ○ ○ ○
   27 28 29 30
   ○ ○ ○ ○
   31 32 33 34

e. moderating a panel discussion with six people

3e ○ ○ ○ ○
   27 28 29 30
   ○ ○ ○ ○
   31 32 33 34

f. multiple-camera O/S shots involving two actors in a soap opera

3f ○ ○ ○ ○
   27 28 29 30
   ○ ○ ○ ○
   31 32 33 34

g. sounds of breathing and skis on snow during a downhill race

3g ○ ○ ○ ○
   27 28 29 30
   ○ ○ ○ ○
   31 32 33 34

h. news anchors who remain seated throughout a studio newscast

3h ○ ○ ○ ○
   27 28 29 30
   ○ ○ ○ ○
   31 32 33 34

P A G E
T O T A L ▢

© 2012 Wadsworth, Cengage Learning

4. When demonstrating a product during a two-camera live show, you should orient the product toward the (35) *close-up camera* (36) *medium-shot camera* and keep looking at the (37) *close-up camera* (38) *medium-shot camera*. **(Fill in two bubbles.)**

5. When demonstrating a small object, you should (39) *hold it as close to the lens as possible* (40) *keep it as steady as possible on the display table* (41) *lift it up for optimal camera pickup*.

6. When you notice that you're looking into the wrong (not switched on-the-air) camera, you should (42) *look down and then up again into the on-the-air camera* (43) *glance immediately over to the on-the-air camera* (44) *keep looking into the wrong camera until it is punched up on the air*.

7. When asked for an audio level, you should (45) *quickly count to 10* (46) *say one sentence with a slightly lower voice than when on the air* (47) *speak with your on-the-air voice until told that the level has been taken*.

8. For the talent the most accurate indicator of the camera's field of view is the (48) *relative distance between talent and camera* (49) *floor manager's cues* (50) *studio monitor*.

9. When wearing a lavalier mic, you should (51) *maintain your voice level regardless of how far the camera is away from you* (52) *increase your volume when the camera gets farther away from you* (53) *speak more softly when the camera is relatively close to you*.

10. When you receive cues during the actual video recording that differ from the rehearsed ones, you should (54) *execute the action as rehearsed* (55) *promptly follow the floor manager's cues* (56) *check with the director*.

11. When making an on-camera announcement in the studio, you should normally take your opening cue from the (57) *camera tally light* (58) *camera operator* (59) *floor manager*.

4	○ 35	○ 36	
	○ 37	○ 38	
5	○ 39	○ 40	○ 41
6	○ 42	○ 43	○ 44
7	○ 45	○ 46	○ 47
8	○ 48	○ 49	○ 50
9	○ 51	○ 52	○ 53
10	○ 54	○ 55	○ 56
11	○ 57	○ 58	○ 59

PAGE TOTAL ⬜

SECTION TOTAL ⬜

© 2012 Wadsworth, Cengage Learning

REVIEW OF ACTING TECHNIQUES

Select the correct answers and fill in the bubbles with the corresponding numbers.

1. When you notice that the boom mic has not quite caught up with you, you should (60) *wait for the mic* (61) *continue with the dialogue* (62) *speak louder.*

2. When repeating action for close-ups (such as drinking a glass of milk), you (63) *use the opportunity to improve on what you have done in the long or medium shots* (64) *get a new glass and have it refilled for each close-up* (65) *use the same props and have your glass filled to the level just before the close-up.*

3. When acting for television, you should project your motions and emotions as you would on the stage (66) *when there is a prolonged dialogue pause* (67) *never* (68) *every time the camera is relatively far away.*

4. When blocked in the camera-far position in an O/S shot, you must make sure that you see the (69) *tally light* (70) *floor manager* (71) *camera lens.*

5. A "blocking map" is (72) *a rough map drawn by the floor manager* (73) *a mental map to remember prominent positions* (74) *the lines drawn on the floor by the AD.*

6. Television plays are video-recorded (75) *in the order of scenes from the beginning to the end of the script* (76) *in brief scenes, grouped by location, characters involved, and so forth* (77) *according to the mood of the director.*

7. When auditioning for a television drama, you should (78) *apply your theatre technique to show that you have stage training* (79) *wear something unusual so the director will remember you* (80) *internalize the role as much as possible.*

8. After the blocking rehearsal with the director, you (81) *can make minor changes if the camera operator concurs* (82) *must keep the exact blocking as rehearsed* (83) *can suggest a different blocking during the video recording.*

9. In a standard studio-recorded daytime serial, the television camera looks at you primarily in (84) *long shots* (85) *close-ups* (86) *low-level shots.*

10. When on a close-up, you should (87) *slow down* (88) *accelerate* (89) *not change* the speed of your on-camera actions.

11. When the camera is relatively far away from you, you should (90) *exaggerate your facial expressions* (91) *exaggerate your gestures* (92) *maintain your close-up acting style.*

1	○ 60	○ 61	○ 62
2	○ 63	○ 64	○ 65
3	○ 66	○ 67	○ 68
4	○ 69	○ 70	○ 71
5	○ 72	○ 73	○ 74
6	○ 75	○ 76	○ 77
7	○ 78	○ 79	○ 80
8	○ 81	○ 82	○ 83
9	○ 84	○ 85	○ 86
10	○ 87	○ 88	○ 89
11	○ 90	○ 91	○ 92

SECTION TOTAL

© 2012 Wadsworth, Cengage Learning

REVIEW OF MAKEUP AND CLOTHING

Select the correct answers and fill in the bubbles with the corresponding numbers.

1. When applying makeup, the ideal lighting conditions are the same as or close to those of (93) *your customary dressing room* (94) *the actual production environment* (95) *normal 3,200K studio lights.*

2. Under high-color-temperature lighting, use (96) *cool* (97) *warm* (98) *neutral* makeup colors.

3. As a weathercaster you can wear green so long as the chroma-key backdrop is (99) *blue* (100) *green* (101) *white.*

4. One of the most widely used makeup foundations is (102) *cake* (103) *grease base* (104) *pan-stick.*

5. When working with a small single-chip camcorder under low-light conditions, you should avoid wearing (105) *red* (106) *green* (107) *blue.*

6. You can counteract a heavy five-o'clock shadow by applying a light layer of (108) *yellow* (109) *skin-colored* (110) *bluish* pan-stick.

7. Clothing with thin, highly contrasting stripes or checkered patterns is (111) *acceptable* (112) *not acceptable* because (113) *the digital camera CCD can handle such a contrast* (114) *it provides exciting patterns* (115) *it causes moiré color vibrations* (116) *it is too detailed for the camera to see.* **(Fill in two bubbles.)**

8. The dress of a pop singer has many rhinestones that sparkle under the colored stage lights. This dress is (117) *acceptable* (118) *not acceptable* because (119) *the color camera can handle small areas of bright light* (120) *there is too much brightness contrast* (121) *it will cause moiré patterns* (122) *it will help raise the baselight level.* **(Fill in two bubbles.)**

1	○ 93	○ 94	○ 95
2	○ 96	○ 97	○ 98
3	○ 99	○ 100	○ 101
4	○ 102	○ 103	○ 104
5	○ 105	○ 106	○ 107
6	○ 108	○ 109	○ 110

7 ○ 111 ○ 112
○ 113 ○ 114 ○ 115 ○ 116

8 ○ 117 ○ 118
○ 119 ○ 120 ○ 121 ○ 122

SECTION TOTAL [ ]

© 2012 Wadsworth, Cengage Learning

REVIEW QUIZ

*Mark the following statements as true or false by filling in the bubbles in the **T** (for true) or*
__F__ (for false) column.

		T	F

1. When asked to give an audio level, you should count quickly to 10.

   1 ○ 123 ○ 124

2. When you are on the air in a dramatic role, you must follow the rehearsed blocking precisely.

   2 ○ 125 ○ 126

3. What you wear when auditioning for a role is unimportant.

   3 ○ 127 ○ 128

4. When you work with a teleprompter, it is best to move the camera as close to the talent as possible.

   4 ○ 129 ○ 130

5. Talent includes both performers and actors.

   5 ○ 131 ○ 132

6. When the camera is relatively far from you, you should walk toward it for good close-ups.

   6 ○ 133 ○ 134

7. In an unrehearsed show, you can give the crew and the director a verbal warning cue of what you are going to do next.

   7 ○ 135 ○ 136

8. When on a close-up, you must pick up the item you are demonstrating and hold it close to the camera lens.

   8 ○ 137 ○ 138

9. When on a panel, you should reposition the desk mic so that it points directly at you.

   9 ○ 139 ○ 140

10. Television actors always portray someone else.

    10 ○ 141 ○ 142

11. To maintain sound perspective, you should talk louder when the camera is farther away from you and more softly when the camera is close to you.

    11 ○ 143 ○ 144

12. When demonstrating a small object, you can help the director by asking that the camera move a little closer.

    12 ○ 145 ○ 146

SECTION
TOTAL ____

© 2012 Wadsworth, Cengage Learning

W-201

PROBLEM-SOLVING APPLICATIONS

1. To practice blocking, write down a series of moves that carry you around your kitchen. For example, you can start at the stove, then get the teakettle out of the cupboard, fill it with water, and put it on the stove, go back to pick up the telephone, put down the telephone to answer the door, and so forth. Try to hit the same marks each time you go through the routine. If possible, have a friend video-record your blocking maneuvers from the same camera position. You can then compare the recordings and check how accurate your blocking was. As part of the same exercise, you can use various props (kitchen utensils) to see how the camera's field of view (LS to ECU) will influence your handling of them.

2. Use a product of your choice and video-record your pitch. What do you like about your performance? What don't you like? How could you improve your performance?

3. Pretend that you, person A, are receiving a telephone call from person B. In this scene we see and hear only person A (you). Using exactly the same dialogue (see the script on the following page), adapt your delivery and acting style to at least two of the following circumstances:

   a. B calls to tell you that he/she has just got an exciting new job.

   b. B calls to tell you that he/she has just lost his/her job.

   c. B has just had an accident with your new car.

   d. B has broken the engagement.

   e. B has won first prize in a video competition.

   Locate the scene anywhere you like. You may do well to write the other part of the phone conversation so that you can "listen" to the virtual B part of the dialogue and respond more convincingly verbally and nonverbally.

4. Have a friend take close-ups of you when you do the phone exercise and compare your expressions when the phone call brings happy news and unhappy news.

5. An experienced stage director, who is directing an adaptation of a stage play for TV, tells the lead actress that her facial expressions are not big enough to "reach the last row." What is your reaction? Be specific.

© 2012 Wadsworth, Cengage Learning

PHONE CONVERSATION

PERSON A

Hello?

Hi.

Fine, and you?

Good.

No.

No, really. It's always good to hear from you.

I beg your pardon?

You must be kidding.

Yes.

No.

What does Alex say to all this?

No. Should I?

I don't know.

Perhaps.

You want me to come over now?

Yes. Really.

Well, this changes things somewhat.

I think so.

I'm not so sure.

Yes. No. I...

All right. But not...

OK.

If you think this is...

Definitely.

Good-bye... When?

No. Really.

Good-bye.

© 2012 Wadsworth, Cengage Learning

The Director in Production

REVIEW OF KEY TERMS

Match each term with its appropriate definition by filling in the corresponding bubble.

1. schedule time
2. intercom
3. camera rehearsal

4. dress rehearsal
5. single-camera directing
6. dry run

7. running time
8. walk-through
9. multicamera directing

A. A communication system widely used by all production and technical personnel so that they can communicate with one another during a show

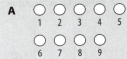

B. Duration of a program or program segment

C. The times when a program starts and stops

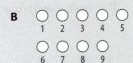

D. A full rehearsal with cameras and other pieces of production equipment

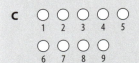

PAGE TOTAL ☐

© 2012 Wadsworth, Cengage Learning

(10) pan right	(15) dolly out	(19) pan left
(11) tilt down	(16) truck right	(20) pedestal down
(12) zoom in	(17) arc left	or crane down
(13) zoom out	(18) pedestal up or	(21) tilt up
(14) dolly in	crane up	

d.

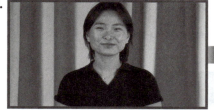

1d
○ ○ ○ ○
10 11 12 13
○ ○ ○ ○
14 15 16 17
○ ○ ○ ○
18 19 20 21

e.

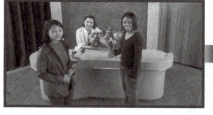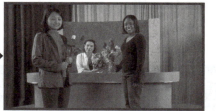

1e
○ ○ ○ ○
10 11 12 13
○ ○ ○ ○
14 15 16 17
○ ○ ○ ○
18 19 20 21

f.

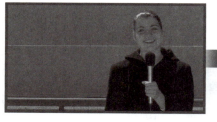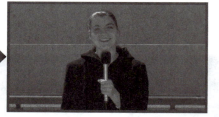

1f
○ ○ ○ ○
10 11 12 13
○ ○ ○ ○
14 15 16 17
○ ○ ○ ○
18 19 20 21

PHOTOS: EDWARD AIONA

P A G E
T O T A L

© 2012 Wadsworth, Cengage Learning

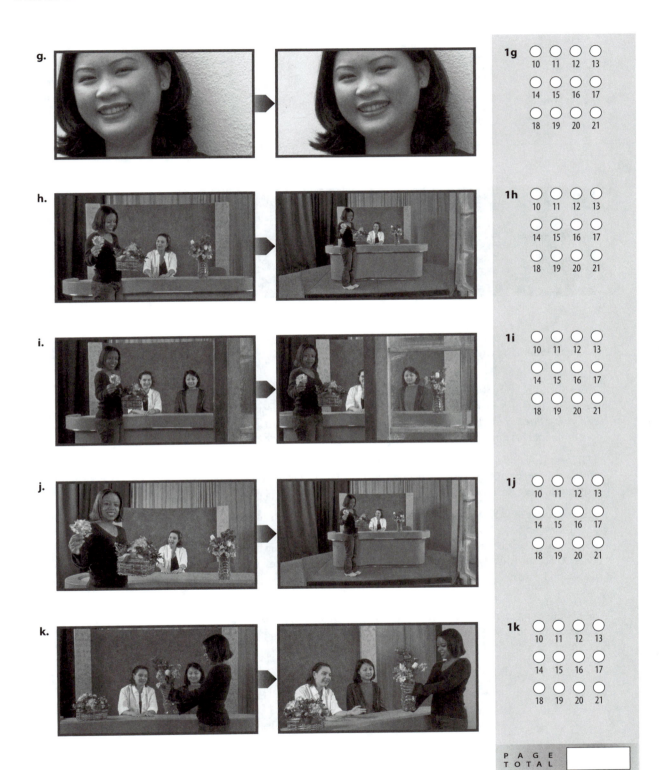

g.

1g	10	11	12	13
	14	15	16	17
	18	19	20	21

h.

1h	10	11	12	13
	14	15	16	17
	18	19	20	21

i.

1i	10	11	12	13
	14	15	16	17
	18	19	20	21

j.

1j	10	11	12	13
	14	15	16	17
	18	19	20	21

k.

1k	10	11	12	13
	14	15	16	17
	18	19	20	21

PAGE TOTAL

PHOTOS: EDWARD AIONA

© 2012 Wadsworth, Cengage Learning

(10) pan right	(15) dolly out	(19) pan left
(11°)tilt down	(16) truck right	(20) pedestal down
(12) zoom in	(17) arc left	or crane down
(13) zoom out	(18) pedestal up or	(21) tilt up
(14) dolly in	crane up	

l.

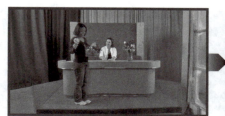 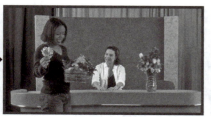

PHOTOS: EDWARD AIONA

1l
○ ○ ○ ○
10 11 12 13
○ ○ ○ ○
14 15 16 17
○ ○ ○ ○
18 19 20 21

2. Director's sequencing cues.

a. From the list below, select the director who uses the correct sequence of cues for the opening of a two-camera (C1 and C2) interview and fill in the corresponding bubble. *(There is a title key for the guest. Assume that the crew has received a general standby cue and that bars and tone have already been recorded on the tape by the AD.)*

(22) *Director A:* "Ready to take C.G. Slate. Take slate. Ready black. Black. Beeper. Ready to come up on one CU of host—take one. Cue host. Ready two [on guest]. Take two. Cue guest. Key title. Take one."

(23) *Director B:* "Ready to roll video recorder. Roll video recorder. Ready C.G. Slate. Take C.G. Read slate. Ready black. Ready beeper. Beeper. To black. Change page [C.G.]. One, CU of host. Ready to come up on one. Open mic, cue host, up on one. Two, CU of guest. Ready two. Ready key C.G. Take two, key. Lose key. Ready one, two-shot. Take one."

(24) *Director C:* "Ready to roll video recorder. Roll video recorder. Ready C.G. Slate. Read slate. Ready black. Ready beeper. To black. Beeper. Ready to come up on one. Up on one. Ready two. Take two. Key. Lose key. Ready one. Take one."

2a
○ ○ ○
22 23 24

PAGE
TOTAL [ ]

© 2012 Wadsworth, Cengage Learning

b. From the list below, select the correct director's cues for transitions by filling in the corresponding bubbles. *(Multiple answers are possible.)*

(25) Ready to take camera two. Take camera two.

(26) Ready three. Take three.

(27) Ready one. Dissolve to one.

(28) Ready to go to black. Go to black.

(29) Ready wipe. Dissolve to two.

(30) Ready to change C.G. page. Change page.

2b ○ 25 ○ 26 ○ 27
○ 28 ○ 29 ○ 30

c. From the list below, select the correct director's cues to the floor manager by filling in the corresponding bubbles. The talent are Mary, Lisa, John, and Larry. *(Multiple answers are possible.)*

(31) Ready to cue Mary. Cue Mary.

(32) Ready to cue him. Cue him.

(33) Make him talk faster.

(34) Move her stage-right.

(35) Turn the sculpture counterclockwise.

(36) Give Lisa the wind-up.

2c ○ 31 ○ 32 ○ 33
○ 34 ○ 35 ○ 36

3. Director's cues to floor manager concerning the positioning of props. Select the appropriate cue to the floor manager to adjust the position of the prop shown on the left screen to that of the right screen and fill in the bubbles with the corresponding numbers.

(37) turn the sculpture counterclockwise
(38) turn the sculpture clockwise

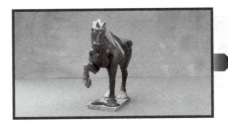 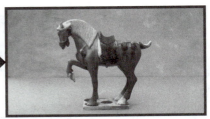

3 ○ 37 ○ 38

P A G E
T O T A L

PHOTOS: HERBERT ZETTL

© 2012 Wadsworth, Cengage Learning

4. **Director's cues to the floor manager concerning the positioning of talent.** From the list below, select the appropriate cue to the floor manager to adjust the position of the talent shown on the left screen to that of the right screen (in pairs **a** through **c**) and fill in the bubbles with the corresponding numbers.

(39) have woman turn to her left
(40) have camera arc right

a.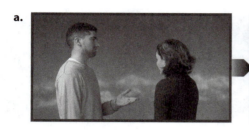

4a ◯ ◯
    39 40

(41) have talent turn in [toward the camera]
(42) have talent move left

b.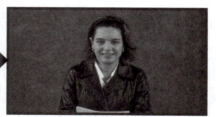

4b ◯ ◯
    41 42

(43) pan right
(44) move talent to camera right

c.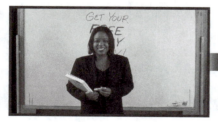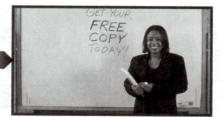

4c ◯ ◯
    43 44

PAGE TOTAL

SECTION TOTAL

PART III   *PRODUCTION*

PHOTOS: EDWARD AIONA

© 2012 Wadsworth, Cengage Learning

REVIEW OF REHEARSAL TECHNIQUES

Select the correct answers and fill in the bubbles with the corresponding numbers.

1. When doing a walk-through/camera rehearsal combination from the studio floor, you should give (45) *only the camera cues* (46) *only the talent cues* (47) *all cues as though you were directing from the control room.*

2. If pressed for time, you should call for (48) *an uninterrupted camera rehearsal* (49) *a walk-through/camera rehearsal combination* (50) *a blocking rehearsal.*

3. Blocking rehearsals are most efficiently conducted from (51) *the control room* (52) *the studio floor or rehearsal hall* (53) *the actual studio set.*

4. When scheduling "notes" segments in your time line, you need to also schedule (54) *additional talent rehearsal time* (55) *reset time* (56) *additional technical rehearsal time.*

5. When engaged in a standard EFP, you need not worry about (57) *talent and technical walk-throughs* (58) *cross-overs from one location to the next* (59) *an extensive intercom setup.*

6. Camera rehearsal is conducted (60) *similar to a dress rehearsal* (61) *for cameras only* (62) *for all technical operations but without talent.*

7. When doing a single-camera ENG or EFP, you should (63) *always get a fair amount of cutaways* (64) *get cutaways only if you think your shots will not cut together well* (65) *not bother with cutaways if you have plenty of time for postproduction.*

8. When calling for a "take," you should pause between the "ready" and the "take" cues (66) *as little as possible* (67) *until you see the TD put his finger on the correct switcher button* (68) *for at least five seconds.*

9. Rehearsals that combine walk-throughs and camera rehearsal are most efficiently conducted from the (69) *studio floor* (70) *rehearsal hall* (71) *control room.*

10. When breaking down an EFP script for a single-camera production, you should (72) *try to maintain the narrative order of the scenes* (73) *combine all scenes that play at the same location and/or with the same talent* (74) *start with the most interesting parts to take advantage of the talent's creative energy.*

1	○ 45	○ 46	○ 47
2	○ 48	○ 49	○ 50
3	○ 51	○ 52	○ 53
4	○ 54	○ 55	○ 56
5	○ 57	○ 58	○ 59
6	○ 60	○ 61	○ 62
7	○ 63	○ 64	○ 65
8	○ 66	○ 67	○ 68
9	○ 69	○ 70	○ 71
10	○ 72	○ 73	○ 74

SECTION TOTAL ☐

© 2012 Wadsworth, Cengage Learning

REVIEW OF MULTICAMERA DIRECTING

1. Assume that the following six shots represent a sequence of video inputs on the preview monitor in the order you will switch them to the line-out. Using the floor plan below, specify the cameras and the other video inputs used for the shots. Note that one video input does not originate in the studio and another uses two video sources simultaneously. (*Multiple answers are possible.*)

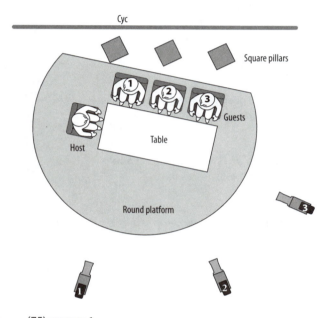

Sources: (75) camera 1

(76) camera 2

(77) camera 3

(78) video recording 1

(79) C.G.

a.

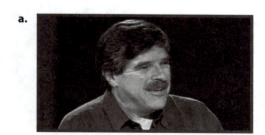

Host

1a ○ ○ ○ ○ ○
    75 76 77 78 79

PAGE
TOTAL

PHOTO: BROADCAST AND ELECTRONIC COMMUNICATION ARTS DEPARTMENT AT SAN FRANCISCO STATE UNIVERSITY

© 2012 Wadsworth, Cengage Learning

b.

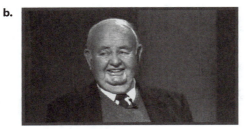

Guest 1

1b ○ ○ ○ ○ ○
75 76 77 78 79

c.

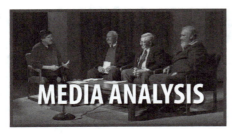

MEDIA ANALYSIS

1c ○ ○ ○ ○ ○
75 76 77 78 79

d.

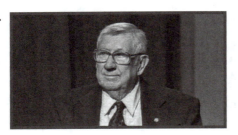

Guest 2

1d ○ ○ ○ ○ ○
75 76 77 78 79

e.

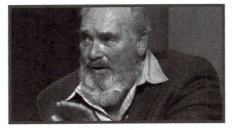

Guest 3

1e ○ ○ ○ ○ ○
75 76 77 78 79

f.

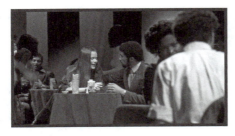

1f ○ ○ ○ ○ ○
75 76 77 78 79

PAGE
TOTAL

SECTION
TOTAL

PHOTOS: BROADCAST AND ELECTRONIC COMMUNICATION ARTS DEPARTMENT AT SAN FRANCISCO STATE UNIVERSITY

© 2012 Wadsworth, Cengage Learning

REVIEW OF TIMING

Select the correct answers and fill in the bubbles with the corresponding numbers.

1. Subjective time refers to (80) *the running time of the show segment* (81) *how fast or slow it seems to move* (82) *how the parts of the segment relate to one another.*

2. In the noon newscast, you must switch to the first 3-minute satellite feed at exactly 3:45 minutes into the show and the second feed at 15:15 minutes after the end of the first one. You need to switch to the remote feeds at:

   (83) 12:03:45 and 12:19:00

   (84) 12:03:45 and 12:22:00

   (85) 12:03:45 and 12:15:15

3. The log indicates that the *Women: Face-to-face* program ends at 11:26:30. A large part of the program is taken up by a fashion show. The fashion coordinator would like a 1-minute, a 30-second, and a 15-second cue, as well as a cut at the end of her segment. The regular program host, who follows the fashion show with a 1½-minute closing, would like a 30-second and a 15-second cue and a cut at the end of the program. From the list below, select the correct clock times for the cues.

   (86) 11:24:00, 11:24:30, 11:24:45, 11:25:00 and 11:26:00, 11:26:15, 11:26:30

   (87) 11:24:30, 11:25:00, 11:25:45, 11:26:00 and 11:26:15, 11:26:30

   (88) 11:22:00, 11:23:00, 11:24:00, 11:24:30 and 11:25:00, 11:26:00, 11:26:15

1	○ 80	○ 81	○ 82
2	○ 83	○ 84	○ 85
3	○ 86	○ 87	○ 88

SECTION
TOTAL

© 2012 Wadsworth, Cengage Learning

REVIEW OF SINGLE-CAMERA DIRECTING

Select the correct answers and fill in the bubbles with the corresponding numbers.

1. When directing single-camera style, you (89) *can visualize each shot independently of all others* (90) *can do away with cutaways* (91) *need to be concerned about continuity of widely dispersed shots.*

1 ○ ○ ○
    89   90   91

2. In single-camera directing, camera placement is (92) *not important because you are shooting from various angles anyway* (93) *very important to ensure continuity* (94) *determined primarily by where the actors are.*

2 ○ ○ ○
    92   93   94

3. When directing single-camera style, you should (95) *rehearse each shot before the take* (96) *rehearse all shots before ever activating the camera* (97) *rehearse the shots in the order of the storyboard narrative.*

3 ○ ○ ○
    95   96   97

4. When directing single-camera style in the studio, you need to rehearse and direct each shot (98) *always from the control room* (99) *always from the studio floor* (100) *from either the control room or the studio floor.*

4 ○ ○ ○
    98   99   100

5. When directing single-camera style in the field, you need (101) *the camera hooked up to a field monitor* (102) *to use the camera viewfinder to correct shots* (103) *neither a field monitor nor a viewfinder.*

5 ○ ○ ○
    101   102   103

6. In single-camera directing, you should slate (104) *each take* (105) *each shot* (106) *each scene.*

6 ○ ○ ○
    104   105   106

7. When recording out of sequence, you will find (107) *a large external viewfinder* (108) *a storyboard* (109) *the PA's notes* especially helpful for your visualization.

7 ○ ○ ○
    107   108   109

SECTION TOTAL [ ]

© 2012 Wadsworth, Cengage Learning

REVIEW QUIZ

*Mark the following statements as true or false by filling in the bubbles in the **T** (for true) or*
***F** (for false) column.*

		T	F
1.	When directing a studio show, the S.A. system is more appropriate than the P.L. system.	1 ○ 110	○ 111
2.	Keeping accurate running time is more important in directing a live multicamera show than a single-camera EFP.	2 ○ 112	○ 113
3.	When directing from the control room, you should address the name of the camera operator rather than the camera number to get efficient camera action.	3 ○ 114	○ 115
4.	During a walk-through/camera rehearsal combination, the director rehearses primarily from the studio floor.	4 ○ 116	○ 117
5.	When directing a fully scripted show, you should pay more attention to the script than the preview or line monitors.	5 ○ 118	○ 119
6.	Even with an efficient intercom system, the switcher should always be located right next to the director's position.	6 ○ 120	○ 121
7.	When directing a daily newscast, you do not need a floor plan to preplan the camera shots.	7 ○ 122	○ 123
8.	You should tell the floor manager whenever there is a technical problem that you need to solve from the control room.	8 ○ 124	○ 125
9.	Even when doing an EFP, you should check the video recording to see whether the preceding scene was properly recorded before moving to the next location.	9 ○ 126	○ 127
10.	To save time in a studio rehearsal, you should use the S.A. system as often as possible.	10 ○ 128	○ 129
11.	When directing a single-camera EFP, a properly working intercom system is one of the most essential setup items.	11 ○ 130	○ 131
12.	When doing an EFP, the talent and technical walk-throughs are less important than when doing a studio show.	12 ○ 132	○ 133
13.	Cutaways are especially important in film-style shooting.	13 ○ 134	○ 135
14.	An external monitor that carries the camera's video greatly facilitates single-camera directing.	14 ○ 136	○ 137
15.	The floor manager's cues are especially important when engaged in single-camera EFP.	15 ○ 138	○ 139

SECTION TOTAL [ ]

© 2012 Wadsworth, Cengage Learning

PROBLEM-SOLVING APPLICATIONS

1. Mark a scene from a fully scripted TV play and practice calling the shots.

2. During the video recording of the first scene of a demanding outdoor EFP for a car commercial, the audio person suggests doing a retake because she picked up a brief, distant jet sound. Would you recommend a retake? If so, why? If not, why not?

3. During the evening news, the wrong video-recorded story comes up. What can you do?

4. During an O/S sequence in a multicamera dramatic production, one of the actors has trouble hitting the blocking marks and is frequently obscured by the camera-near person. What advice would you give the actor?

5. Get a published script of an episode of a drama or soap opera and mark it for three-camera and single-camera directing.

6. The director uses one set of commands during rehearsal but switches to another when doing the on-the-air show. Which potential problems do you foresee, if any? Be specific.

7. The producer suggests that you should not waste valuable time by doing a walk-through/camera rehearsal from the studio floor but skip right to the camera rehearsal from the control room. What is your reaction? Why?

8. When checking all the intercom systems before a remote live multicamera telecast of a large political gathering at city hall, the talent's I.F.B. interrupts itself from time to time. What backup cueing device would you recommend that close to airtime?

9. When pressed for time, the director decides to conduct the rehearsal from the studio floor. Would you agree or disagree with such a move? Be specific. How, if at all, would the director's request affect the studio equipment and the control room activities?

10. The floor manager expresses her concern to you, the director, about the lack of adequate intercom facilities for an EFP of the local garden show. How would you respond?

11. The line producer of a complex commercial considers the director's explaining the process message to talent and crew a waste of time. What is your reaction? Be specific.

© 2012 Wadsworth, Cengage Learning

Course No. _____ Date _____ Name _____

Field Production and Big Remotes

REVIEW OF KEY TERMS

Match each term with its appropriate definition by filling in the corresponding bubble.

1. broadband
2. direct broadcast satellite
3. downlink
4. microwave relay
5. remote survey
6. iso camera
7. mini-link
8. field production
9. big remote
10. instant replay
11. Ku-band
12. uplink

A. A variety of information sent simultaneously over a fiber-optic cable

A ① ② ③ ④
⑤ ⑥ ⑦ ⑧
⑨ ⑩ ⑪ ⑫

B. A signal transport from the remote location to the station or transmitter in various transmission steps

B ① ② ③ ④
⑤ ⑥ ⑦ ⑧
⑨ ⑩ ⑪ ⑫

C. Repeating a key play or an important event for the viewer, through playing back by videotape or disk-stored video, immediately after its live occurrence

C ① ② ③ ④
⑤ ⑥ ⑦ ⑧
⑨ ⑩ ⑪ ⑫

P A G E
T O T A L

© 2012 Wadsworth, Cengage Learning

CHAPTER 18   FIELD PRODUCTION AND BIG REMOTES

W-221

REVIEW OF FIELD PRODUCTION

Select the correct answers and fill in the bubbles with the corresponding numbers.

1. Instant replays are most common in (13) *big remotes* (14) *EFP* (15) *ENG.*

2. Using multiple cameras or camcorders in EFP means that they (16) *shoot a scene simultaneously* (17) *must feed a switcher* (18) *run in sync.*

3. The most flexible type of field production that needs little or no preproduction is (19) *ENG* (20) *EFP* (21) *big remotes.*

4. The walk-through rehearsal is least important for (22) *ENG* (23) *EFP* (24) *big remotes.*

5. A floor manager is most important in (25) *ENG* (26) *EFP* (27) *big remotes.*

6. The directing procedure that most closely resembles multicamera studio production is (28) *ENG* (29) *EFP* (30) *big remotes.*

7. The field production that affords the most control over the event is (31) *ENG* (32) *EFP* (33) *big remotes.*

8. The remote system least likely to use signal transmission equipment is (34) *ENG* (35) *EFP* (36) *big remotes.*

9. A complex intercommunication system is most important for (37) *ENG* (38) *EFP* (39) *big remotes.*

10. Because the camera setup is done by technical personnel, the director is (40) *not needed* (41) *very important* (42) *consulted only in emergencies* for the specific locations of the key cameras.

11. A big-remote survey requires (43) *only a production survey* (44) *only a technical survey* (45) *both a production and a technical survey.*

12. The normal transmission equipment in ENG vans is (46) *a microwave transmitter* (47) *a satellite uplink* (48) *fiber-optic cable.*

13. To ensure access to the event location, you need (49) *a contact person* (50) *a written statement from the producer* (51) *an OK from the chief of police.*

14. The field production that almost always requires careful postproduction is (52) *ENG* (53) *big remotes* (54) *EFP.*

1	○ 13	○ 14	○ 15
2	○ 16	○ 17	○ 18
3	○ 19	○ 20	○ 21
4	○ 22	○ 23	○ 24
5	○ 25	○ 26	○ 27
6	○ 28	○ 29	○ 30
7	○ 31	○ 32	○ 33
8	○ 34	○ 35	○ 36
9	○ 37	○ 38	○ 39
10	○ 40	○ 41	○ 42
11	○ 43	○ 44	○ 45
12	○ 46	○ 47	○ 48
13	○ 49	○ 50	○ 51
14	○ 52	○ 53	○ 54

SECTION TOTAL

© 2012 Wadsworth, Cengage Learning

REVIEW OF BIG REMOTES

1. Analyze the following five location sketches for field productions and big remotes. Evaluate the type and the position of each camera by the criteria listed below and fill in the bubbles with the corresponding numbers. *(Multiple answers are possible.)*

   (55) camera position OK
   (56) wrong or unnecessary camera position
   (57) inappropriate camera type
   (58) cable hazard
   (59) lighting problems (shooting into the sun or against another strong light source)

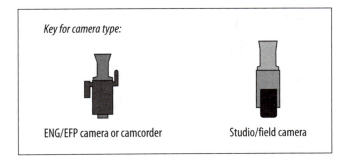

Key for camera type:

ENG/EFP camera or camcorder   Studio/field camera

(55) camera position OK
(56) wrong or unnecessary camera position
(57) inappropriate camera type
(58) cable hazard
(59) lighting problems (shooting into the sun or against another strong light source)

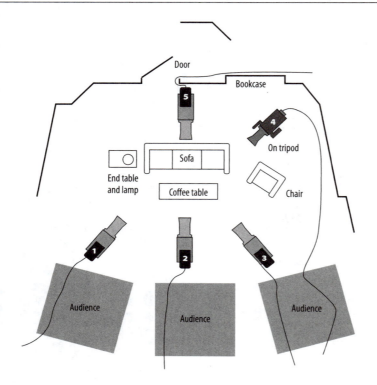

Play

Video recording of two performances of a high-school play (situation comedy) with a live audience, minimal postproduction, and the use of a large remote truck

    a. comments on C1

    b. comments on C2

    c. comments on C3

    d. comments on C4

    e. comments on C5

1a **C1** ○ ○ ○
     55 56 57
     ○ ○
     58 59

1b **C2** ○ ○ ○
     55 56 57
     ○ ○
     58 59

1c **C3** ○ ○ ○
     55 56 57
     ○ ○
     58 59

1d **C4** ○ ○ ○
     55 56 57
     ○ ○
     58 59

1e **C5** ○ ○ ○
     55 56 57
     ○ ○
     58 59

P A G E T O T A L [ ]

© 2012 Wadsworth, Cengage Learning

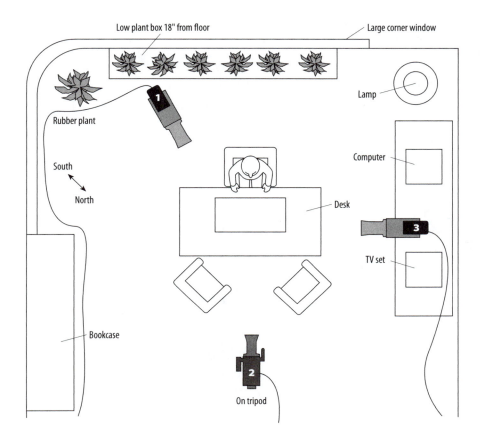

Low plant box 18" from floor

Large corner window

Rubber plant

South

North

Lamp

Computer

Desk

TV set

Bookcase

On tripod

EFP of Company President's Address to Employees
Live-recorded for minimal postproduction
Recording date: July 15
Recording time: 2:30 p.m. to 4:30 p.m.
Place: President's office, Tower Building, 34th floor

    f. comments on C1

    g. comments on C2

    h. comments on C3

1f C1 ◯ ◯ ◯
      55 56 57
      ◯ ◯
      58 59

1g C2 ◯ ◯ ◯
      55 56 57
      ◯ ◯
      58 59

1h C3 ◯ ◯ ◯
      55 56 57
      ◯ ◯
      58 59

PAGE TOTAL

© 2012 Wadsworth, Cengage Learning

(55) camera position OK
(56) wrong or unnecessary camera position
(57) inappropriate camera type
(58) cable hazard
(59) lighting problems (shooting into the sun or against another strong light source)

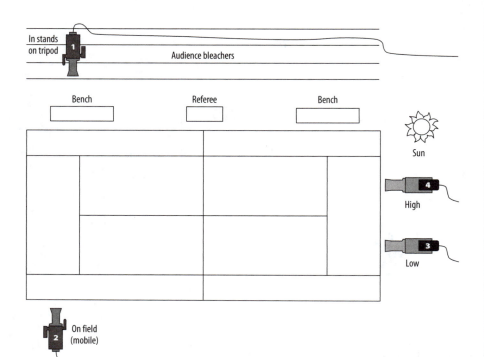

Tennis Match
Live coverage of tennis match

    i. comments on C1

    j. comments on C2

    k. comments on C3

    l. comments on C4

1i C1 ◯ ◯ ◯
         55 56 57
        ◯ ◯
        58 59

1j C2 ◯ ◯ ◯
         55 56 57
        ◯ ◯
        58 59

1k C3 ◯ ◯ ◯
         55 56 57
        ◯ ◯
        58 59

1l C4 ◯ ◯ ◯
         55 56 57
        ◯ ◯
        58 59

P A G E
T O T A L

© 2012 Wadsworth, Cengage Learning

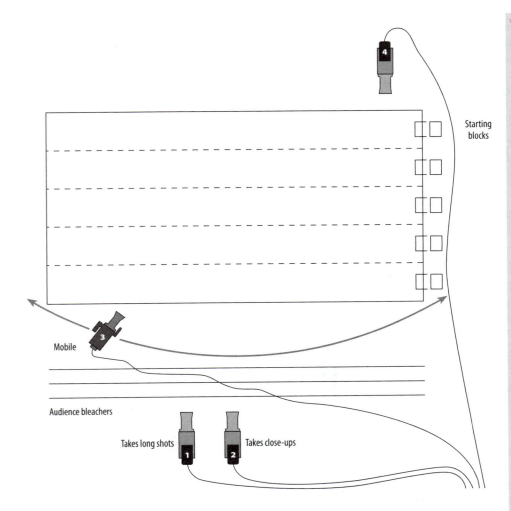

Starting blocks

Mobile

Audience bleachers

Takes long shots

Takes close-ups

Swim Meet

Live telecast of state swim meet; large indoor pool

    m. comments on C1

    n. comments on C2

    o. comments on C3

    p. comments on C4

1m C1 ○ ○ ○
      55 56 57
      ○ ○
      58 59

1n C2 ○ ○ ○
      55 56 57
      ○ ○
      58 59

1o C3 ○ ○ ○
      55 56 57
      ○ ○
      58 59

1p C4 ○ ○ ○
      55 56 57
      ○ ○
      58 59

P A G E
T O T A L ☐

© 2012 Wadsworth, Cengage Learning

W-229

(55) camera position OK
(56) wrong or unnecessary camera position
(57) inappropriate camera type
(58) cable hazard
(59) lighting problems (shooting into the sun or against another strong light source)

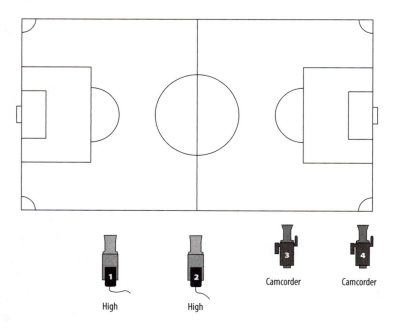

High   High   Camcorder   Camcorder

Soccer Practice

EFP of soccer practice for a show that demonstrates the beauty and the grace of a soccer game; heavy postproduction with effects and sound track

q. comments on C1

r. comments on C2

s. comments on C3

t. comments on C4

1q C1 ○ ○ ○
        55 56 57
        ○ ○
        58 59

1r C2 ○ ○ ○
        55 56 57
        ○ ○
        58 59

1s C3 ○ ○ ○
        55 56 57
        ○ ○
        58 59

1t C4 ○ ○ ○
        55 56 57
        ○ ○
        58 59

P A G E
T O T A L [   ]

SECTION
TOTAL [   ]

© 2012 Wadsworth, Cengage Learning

REVIEW OF FACILITIES REQUESTS

*Evaluate the equipment facilities requests for the three EFPs described below. Identify the **wrong** equipment and the items **not** needed and fill in the bubbles with the corresponding numbers. **Multiple answers are possible.***

1. Live stand-up traffic report from downtown during the afternoon rush hour

   Facilities Request 1
   (60) camcorder
   (61) 2 video recorders
   (62) shotgun mic (camera mic)
   (63) hand mic
   (64) 3 portable lighting kits
   (65) audiotape recorder
   (66) microwave transmission equipment
   (67) I.F.B. intercom
   (68) C.G.

2. Midmorning recording of a brief dance number in front of city hall for a music video using ENG/EFP cameras, *not* camcorders

   Facilities Request 2
   (69) 3 video recorders
   (70) 6 shotgun mics
   (71) ESS
   (72) 3 ENG/EFP cameras
   (73) 3 RCUs, connecting cables, and portable monitors
   (74) large audio mixer
   (75) portable lighting kit
   (76) P.A. audiotape playback system
   (77) C.G.

3. Taped interview of a media scholar in his hotel room for news item

   Facilities Request 3
   (78) camcorder
   (79) iso video recorder
   (80) portable lighting kit
   (81) RCU
   (82) 2 lavalier mics
   (83) portable audio mixer
   (84) recording media
   (85) batteries
   (86) preview monitors

1 ○ ○ ○ ○ ○
     60 61 62 63 64
     ○ ○ ○ ○
     65 66 67 68

2 ○ ○ ○ ○ ○
     69 70 71 72 73
     ○ ○ ○ ○
     74 75 76 77

3 ○ ○ ○ ○ ○
     78 79 80 81 82
     ○ ○ ○ ○
     83 84 85 86

SECTION TOTAL [   ]

© 2012 Wadsworth, Cengage Learning

REVIEW OF SIGNAL TRANSPORT SYSTEMS

Select the correct answers and fill in the bubbles with the corresponding numbers.

1. When stringing cables is prohibited, an EFP camera can use (87) *its own small transmitter* (88) *a C-band uplink* (89) *a Ku-band satellite* to transmit its signal over short distances.

2. The C-band uplink and downlink dishes are (90) *the same as* (91) *smaller than* (92) *larger than* the ones for the Ku-band.

3. A mini-link refers to (93) *a small uplink* (94) *a small downlink* (95) *several microwave links* to transport the signal around an obstacle.

4. A microwave signal (96) *can* (97) *cannot* be blocked by big buildings or mountains.

5. EFP makes (98) *more-frequent use of satellite transmission than* (99) *less-frequent use of satellite transmission than* (100) *about the same amount of satellite transmission as* big remotes.

6. Small uplink trucks use (101) *the Ku-band* (102) *the C-band* (103) *their own satellite frequency* for signal transmission.

7. The Ku-band operates on a frequency that is (104) *higher than* (105) *lower than* (106) *the same as* the frequency for the C-band and is (107) *more stable in bad weather* (108) *less stable in bad weather* (109) *immune to weather conditions*. **(Fill in two bubbles.)**

1	○ 87	○ 88	○ 89
2	○ 90	○ 91	○ 92
3	○ 93	○ 94	○ 95
4	○ 96	○ 97	
5	○ 98	○ 99	○ 100
6	○ 101	○ 102	○ 103
7	○ 104	○ 105	○ 106
	○ 107	○ 108	○ 109

SECTION
TOTAL [ ]

© 2012 Wadsworth, Cengage Learning

REVIEW QUIZ

*Mark the following statements as true or false by filling in the bubbles in the **T** (for true) or **F** (for false) column.*

		T	F
1.	Cameras used for the regular coverage of a remote telecast cannot be used for instant replay.	1 ○ 110	○ 111
2.	A careful audio setup is as important as the camera setup in big remotes.	2 ○ 112	○ 113
3.	Big remote trucks usually contain an audio control, a video-recording control, a program control, and a technical control with signal transmission equipment.	3 ○ 114	○ 115
4.	You need a switcher when using three EFP cameras as multiple isos.	4 ○ 116	○ 117
5.	When shooting single-camera EFP for postproduction, you do not need extensive intercom systems.	5 ○ 118	○ 119
6.	So long as you use an I.F.B. system, the floor manager is unnecessary for big remotes.	6 ○ 120	○ 121
7.	The contact person is important only in preproduction.	7 ○ 122	○ 123
8.	So long as you have a good transmission system, you do not need video recorders in the remote truck.	8 ○ 124	○ 125
9.	Remote surveys are relatively unimportant for ENG.	9 ○ 126	○ 127
10.	The C.G. operation is especially important during a live broadcast of a football game.	10 ○ 128	○ 129
11.	To make the remote telecast as exciting as possible, you should use as many cameras as are available.	11 ○ 130	○ 131
12.	So long as you have good headsets, you do not need other intercom systems on big remotes.	12 ○ 132	○ 133
13.	If possible, you should do the survey for an outdoor remote during the time the actual production will take place.	13 ○ 134	○ 135
14.	Remote surveys are relatively unimportant for EFP.	14 ○ 136	○ 137

SECTION TOTAL [ ]

© 2012 Wadsworth, Cengage Learning

PROBLEM-SOLVING APPLICATIONS

1. To get a good overhead shot of a parade, you, the director, would like to place one of the cameras on the balcony of a twentieth-floor window of a nearby hotel. The TD informs you that the hotel manager has nothing against your renting the room for the day and setting up the camera, but she will not allow any cable runs either inside or outside the hotel. What would you suggest?

2. The producer learns at the last minute that the president of the European Union will arrive at the international airport and wants you to cover her arrival live. According to the producer, you should have no problem with the transmission because the station's transmitter is in line-of-sight of the airport. What field production method would you recommend? Specifically, what equipment and personnel would you need to accomplish this assignment?

3. You are the director for the live multicamera coverage of a large computer convention. While you're giving instructions to the talent to wind up her interview with one of the computer experts, her I.F.B. fails. How else can you communicate with her while she is on the air?

4. Conduct a detailed remote survey for the live coverage of one of the following: (1) a football game, (2) a track meet, (3) a basketball game, (4) a baseball game, (5) a concert of a symphony orchestra, (6) an outdoor rock concert, or (7) a modern dance performance in a city park. Be sure to include all major production items, such as camera placement, audio and lighting requirements, intercom and transmission systems, power source, and so forth.

5. Prepare location sketches and facilities requests for the remote or EFP selected in the previous question.

© 2012 Wadsworth, Cengage Learning

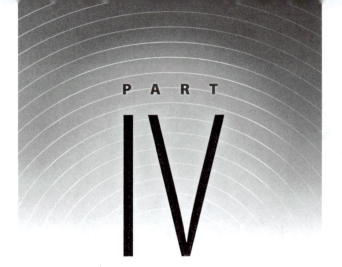

PART IV

Postproduction

© 2012 Wadsworth, Cengage Learning

Postproduction Editing: How It Works

REVIEW OF KEY TERMS

Match each term with its appropriate definition by filling in the corresponding bubble.

1. clip
2. source media
3. vector
4. linear editing
5. off-line editing
6. on-line editing

7. capture
8. edit master recording
9. split edit
10. NLE
11. window dub
12. ADR

13. slate
14. shot
15. time code
16. take
17. EDL
18. VR log

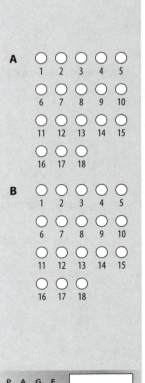

A. Consists of edit-in and edit-out points expressed in time code numbers

A
```
1  2  3  4  5
6  7  8  9  10
11 12 13 14 15
16 17 18
```

B. Editing that uses tape-based systems

B
```
1  2  3  4  5
6  7  8  9  10
11 12 13 14 15
16 17 18
```

PAGE TOTAL [   ]

© 2012 Wadsworth, Cengage Learning

1. clip	7. capture	13. slate
2. source media	8. edit master recording	14. shot
3. vector	9. split edit	15. time code
4. linear editing	10. NLE	16. take
5. off-line editing	11. window dub	17. EDL
6. on-line editing	12. ADR	18. VR log

C. The interval between two transitions

D. A "bumped-down" copy of all source recordings with the time code keyed over each frame

E. A perceivable force with a direction and a magnitude

F. Recapturing the assembled shots at a higher resolution or creating a high-quality edit master tape

PAGE TOTAL

© 2012 Wadsworth, Cengage Learning

G. Process that produces the EDL, a videotape not used for broadcast, or low-resolution capture

G ① ② ③ ④ ⑤
   1 2 3 4 5
   ⑥ ⑦ ⑧ ⑨ ⑩
   6 7 8 9 10
   ⑪ ⑫ ⑬ ⑭ ⑮
   11 12 13 14 15
   ⑯ ⑰ ⑱
   16 17 18

H. Transferring of video and audio information to a computer hard drive

H ① ② ③ ④ ⑤
   1 2 3 4 5
   ⑥ ⑦ ⑧ ⑨ ⑩
   6 7 8 9 10
   ⑪ ⑫ ⑬ ⑭ ⑮
   11 12 13 14 15
   ⑯ ⑰ ⑱
   16 17 18

I. Similar repeated shots taken during video recording or filming

I ① ② ③ ④ ⑤
   1 2 3 4 5
   ⑥ ⑦ ⑧ ⑨ ⑩
   6 7 8 9 10
   ⑪ ⑫ ⑬ ⑭ ⑮
   11 12 13 14 15
   ⑯ ⑰ ⑱
   16 17 18

J. Allows instant random access to and easy rearrangement of shots

J ① ② ③ ④ ⑤
   1 2 3 4 5
   ⑥ ⑦ ⑧ ⑨ ⑩
   6 7 8 9 10
   ⑪ ⑫ ⑬ ⑭ ⑮
   11 12 13 14 15
   ⑯ ⑰ ⑱
   16 17 18

K. A shot or brief sequence of shots captured on the hard drive

K ① ② ③ ④ ⑤
   1 2 3 4 5
   ⑥ ⑦ ⑧ ⑨ ⑩
   6 7 8 9 10
   ⑪ ⑫ ⑬ ⑭ ⑮
   11 12 13 14 15
   ⑯ ⑰ ⑱
   16 17 18

P A G E
T O T A L [   ]

© 2012 Wadsworth, Cengage Learning

1. clip	7. capture	13. slate
2. source media	8. edit master recording	14. shot
3. vector	9. split edit	15. time code
4. linear editing	10. NLE	16. take
5. off-line editing	11. window dub	17. EDL
6. on-line editing	12. ADR	18. VR log

L. Audio precedes the shot or bleeds into the next one

L
○ ○ ○ ○ ○
1 2 3 4 5
○ ○ ○ ○ ○
6 7 8 9 10
○ ○ ○ ○ ○
11 12 13 14 15
○ ○ ○
16 17 18

M. The media that contains the final on-line edit

M
○ ○ ○ ○ ○
1 2 3 4 5
○ ○ ○ ○ ○
6 7 8 9 10
○ ○ ○ ○ ○
11 12 13 14 15
○ ○ ○
16 17 18

N. The recording devices (videotape, hard disk, optical disc, or memory card) that hold the recorded material

N
○ ○ ○ ○ ○
1 2 3 4 5
○ ○ ○ ○ ○
6 7 8 9 10
○ ○ ○ ○ ○
11 12 13 14 15
○ ○ ○
16 17 18

O. A list of all consecutive shots recorded during a production with in and out time code numbers and other information

O
○ ○ ○ ○ ○
1 2 3 4 5
○ ○ ○ ○ ○
6 7 8 9 10
○ ○ ○ ○ ○
11 12 13 14 15
○ ○ ○
16 17 18

P A G E
T O T A L

© 2012 Wadsworth, Cengage Learning

P. A device that provides essential production information recorded at the beginning of each take

P ① ② ③ ④ ⑤
   1 2 3 4 5
   ⑥ ⑦ ⑧ ⑨ ⑩
   6 7 8 9 10
   ⑪ ⑫ ⑬ ⑭ ⑮
   11 12 13 14 15
   ⑯ ⑰ ⑱
   16 17 18

Q. The synchronization of speech with the lip movements of the speaker in postproduction

Q ① ② ③ ④ ⑤
   1 2 3 4 5
   ⑥ ⑦ ⑧ ⑨ ⑩
   6 7 8 9 10
   ⑪ ⑫ ⑬ ⑭ ⑮
   11 12 13 14 15
   ⑯ ⑰ ⑱
   16 17 18

R. Gives each video frame a specific address

R ① ② ③ ④ ⑤
   1 2 3 4 5
   ⑥ ⑦ ⑧ ⑨ ⑩
   6 7 8 9 10
   ⑪ ⑫ ⑬ ⑭ ⑮
   11 12 13 14 15
   ⑯ ⑰ ⑱
   16 17 18

PAGE TOTAL [ ]

SECTION TOTAL [ ]

© 2012 Wadsworth, Cengage Learning

16. Fill in the bubbles whose numbers correspond with the appropriate features of the generic nonlinear editing interface as shown in the following figure:

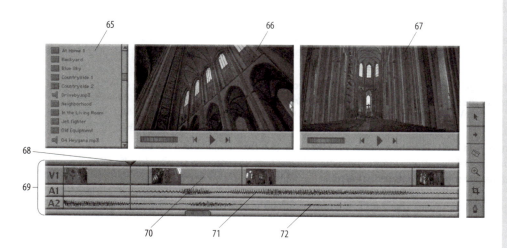

PHOTOS: HERBERT ZETTL

a. time line

b. playhead and scrubber bar

c. video track

d. audio track 1

e. audio track 2

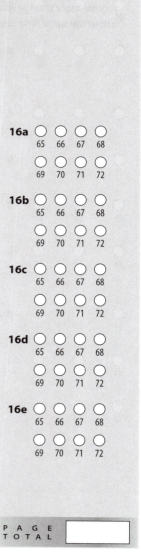

16a ○ ○ ○ ○
     65 66 67 68
     ○ ○ ○ ○
     69 70 71 72

16b ○ ○ ○ ○
     65 66 67 68
     ○ ○ ○ ○
     69 70 71 72

16c ○ ○ ○ ○
     65 66 67 68
     ○ ○ ○ ○
     69 70 71 72

16d ○ ○ ○ ○
     65 66 67 68
     ○ ○ ○ ○
     69 70 71 72

16e ○ ○ ○ ○
     65 66 67 68
     ○ ○ ○ ○
     69 70 71 72

P A G E
T O T A L

© 2012 Wadsworth, Cengage Learning

f. project panel

16f ○ ○ ○ ○
65 66 67 68
○ ○ ○ ○
69 70 71 72

g. record monitor

16g ○ ○ ○ ○
65 66 67 68
○ ○ ○ ○
69 70 71 72

h. source monitor

16h ○ ○ ○ ○
65 66 67 68
○ ○ ○ ○
69 70 71 72

P A G E
T O T A L

SECTION
TOTAL

© 2012 Wadsworth, Cengage Learning

REVIEW OF LINEAR EDITING

Select the correct answers and fill in the bubbles with the corresponding numbers.

1. When using SMPTE time code, you (73) *can* (74) *cannot* add it later over existing source tapes; it (75) *does* (76) *does not* necessarily show the actual time during which the production took place. (***Fill in two bubbles.***)

2. Identify mistakes in the pulse-count display in this figure and fill in the bubbles with the corresponding numbers. (***Multiple answers are possible.***)

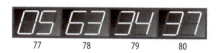

77   78   79   80

3. Select the correct pulse-count display that exhibits the actual edit-in point of the edit master tape shown in the following figure and fill in the bubble with the corresponding number.

Tape is 15:25 minutes in from start

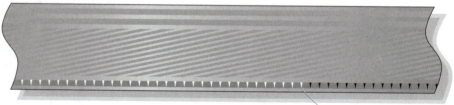

Edit-in point

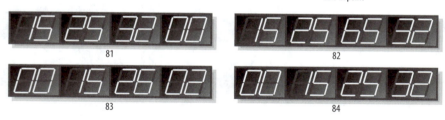

4. The operational principle of linear editing is (85) *file management* (86) *transferring data from a VTR to a hard drive* (87) *copying selected portions of the source tapes.*

5. In the assemble editing mode, the record VTR (88) *will* (89) *will not* copy the control track of the source tape, so you (90) *need* (91) *do not need* to prerecord a continuous control track on the edit master tape. (***Fill in two bubbles.***)

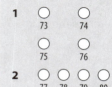

1 ◯ 73   ◯ 74
   ◯ 75   ◯ 76

2 ◯ 77 ◯ 78 ◯ 79 ◯ 80

3 ◯ 81 ◯ 82 ◯ 83 ◯ 84

4 ◯ 85   ◯ 86   ◯ 87

5 ◯ 88   ◯ 89
   ◯ 90   ◯ 91

SECTION TOTAL [　　　]

© 2012 Wadsworth, Cengage Learning

REVIEW QUIZ

*Mark the following statements as true or false by filling in the bubbles in the **T** (for true) or*
__F__ (for false) column.

	T	F

1. If your source tapes are digital, they don't have to be dubbed to the hard drive of an NLE.   **1** ◯ 92 ◯ 93

2. Offline editing in NLE means to initially import the source material into the NLE system at a relatively high compression ratio.   **2** ◯ 94 ◯ 95

3. You can use the AB-roll concept of linear editing in nonlinear editing as well.   **3** ◯ 96 ◯ 97

4. A split edit in nonlinear editing refers to editing audio separately from video.   **4** ◯ 98 ◯ 99

5. In nonlinear editing, the video and audio frames are not actually sequenced but told by the NLE in what order to play back.   **5** ◯ 100 ◯ 101

6. The vector column in a good VR log can show the screen direction of somebody's gaze or movement.   **6** ◯ 102 ◯ 103

7. Linear editing can be done only with VTRs.   **7** ◯ 104 ◯ 105

8. The less compression of video and audio files, the more storage space they require.   **8** ◯ 106 ◯ 107

9. Linear editing works on the same basic principle as nonlinear editing.   **9** ◯ 108 ◯ 109

10. Changing the shot sequence in the middle of a videotape is difficult regardless of whether the information is analog or digital.   **10** ◯ 110 ◯ 111

11. Linear editing can be done only when the source tapes hold analog material.   **11** ◯ 112 ◯ 113

12. Off-line linear editing means that lower-quality equipment is used.   **12** ◯ 114 ◯ 115

13. All NLE systems offer at least two audio tracks.   **13** ◯ 116 ◯ 117

14. Linear editing equipment allows random access to the source material.   **14** ◯ 118 ◯ 119

15. You can add time code to videotape as late as postproduction.   **15** ◯ 120 ◯ 121

16. Contrary to linear editing, an EDL is not practical for nonlinear editing.   **16** ◯ 122 ◯ 123

17. The principle of nonlinear editing is file management.   **17** ◯ 124 ◯ 125

18. Replacing a brief clip sequence in the middle of an edited project is quite difficult and time consuming in nonlinear editing.   **18** ◯ 126 ◯ 127

SECTION TOTAL [____]

© 2012 Wadsworth, Cengage Learning

PROBLEM-SOLVING APPLICATIONS

1. The news producer tells you, the editor, not to bother with an audio transcription of the recent two-hour interview with the mayor because he needs only about 20 seconds of a few memorable sound bites. What is your reaction? Why?

2. The novice director warns you, the editor, that the new client is known to change her mind frequently and may require substantive editing changes right in the middle of the show. The director is worried that such major changes may cause serious time delays. Assuming that you are working with a nonlinear editing system, what would you tell the director? Be specific.

3. The same director tells you to be sure to capture all source tapes at the highest resolution even for an off-line rough-cut because "once in the computer, you are stuck with what you imported." What is your reaction? Why?

4. Even with your new nonlinear editing system, it is cumbersome to find shots that show the new car model traveling in specific screen directions. The producer suggests that you note the various vectors when logging the source footage. What does she mean? How can doing this help you locate the desired shots?

5. The director is a big fan of nonlinear editing because fixing mistakes in postproduction is "now a snap." What is your reaction? Give specific examples.

6. The producer hands you a number of source media from a nature videographer. The program idea is to match the video of the movement of various wild animals to the tempo and the feel of some classical music pieces. He wants you to especially emphasize and juxtapose shots in which the animals move in opposite directions—much like the music. Which logging element would facilitate your editing job?

© 2012 Wadsworth, Cengage Learning

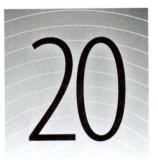

Editing Functions and Principles

REVIEW OF KEY TERMS

Match each term with its appropriate definition by filling in the corresponding bubble.

1. continuity editing
2. vector
3. vector line
4. graphic vector

5. jump cut
6. motion vector
7. complexity editing
8. mental map

9. cutaway
10. montage
11. index vector

A. A shot that is inserted to facilitate continuity

A
○ ○ ○ ○
1 2 3 4
○ ○ ○ ○
5 6 7 8
○ ○ ○
9 10 11

B. A vector created by someone looking or something pointing unquestionably in a specific direction

B
○ ○ ○ ○
1 2 3 4
○ ○ ○ ○
5 6 7 8
○ ○ ○
9 10 11

C. The preservation of visual continuity from shot to shot

C
○ ○ ○ ○
1 2 3 4
○ ○ ○ ○
5 6 7 8
○ ○ ○
9 10 11

PAGE
TOTAL _____

© 2012 Wadsworth, Cengage Learning

1. continuity editing
2. vector
3. vector line
4. graphic vector
5. jump cut
6. motion vector
7. complexity editing
8. mental map
9. cutaway
10. montage
11. index vector

D. The juxtaposition of two or more shots to generate a third overall idea, which may not be contained in any one

D
○ ○ ○ ○
1 2 3 4
○ ○ ○ ○
5 6 7 8
○ ○ ○
9 10 11

E. A perceivable force with a direction and a magnitude

E
○ ○ ○ ○
1 2 3 4
○ ○ ○ ○
5 6 7 8
○ ○ ○
9 10 11

F. The juxtaposition of shots that helps intensify the screen event

F
○ ○ ○ ○
1 2 3 4
○ ○ ○ ○
5 6 7 8
○ ○ ○
9 10 11

G. Juxtaposing shots that violate the established continuity

G
○ ○ ○ ○
1 2 3 4
○ ○ ○ ○
5 6 7 8
○ ○ ○
9 10 11

H. Established by two people facing each other or through a prominent movement in a specific direction

H
○ ○ ○ ○
1 2 3 4
○ ○ ○ ○
5 6 7 8
○ ○ ○
9 10 11

PAGE
TOTAL

© 2012 Wadsworth, Cengage Learning

I. Virtual image of where things are or are supposed to be in on- and off-screen space

I   ○ ○ ○ ○
    1 2 3 4
    ○ ○ ○ ○
    5 6 7 8
    ○ ○ ○
    9 10 11

J. Created by an object actually moving or perceived as moving on-screen

J   ○ ○ ○ ○
    1 2 3 4
    ○ ○ ○ ○
    5 6 7 8
    ○ ○ ○
    9 10 11

K. Created by lines or by stationary elements in such a way as to suggest a line

K   ○ ○ ○ ○
    1 2 3 4
    ○ ○ ○ ○
    5 6 7 8
    ○ ○ ○
    9 10 11

PAGE TOTAL ☐

SECTION TOTAL ☐

© 2012 Wadsworth, Cengage Learning

REVIEW OF CONTINUITY EDITING PRINCIPLES

Select the correct answers and fill in the bubbles with the corresponding numbers.

1. You are given a storyboard to assist you in your single-camera EFP of a conversation between a man and a woman (see the following figure). For each storyboard pair, indicate whether the shots (12) *can* (13) *cannot* be edited together, assuming normal continuity-editing principles.

a.

b.

c.

d.

e.

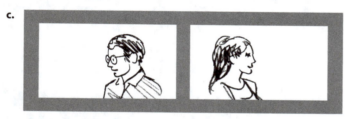
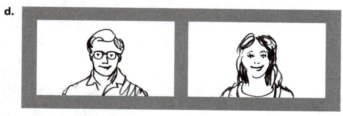
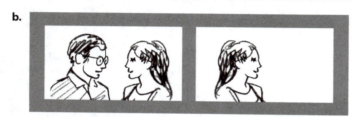
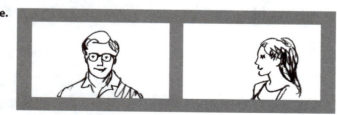

1a ○ ○
   12 13

1b ○ ○
   12 13

1c ○ ○
   12 13

1d ○ ○
   12 13

1e ○ ○
   12 13

PAGE
TOTAL

© 2012 Wadsworth, Cengage Learning

2. From the screen images below (repeated on the following page), select the sequence pair you would get when cutting from camera 1 to camera 2 as shown in the diagrams of the camera positions.

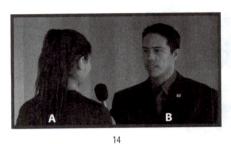
14

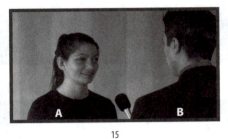
15

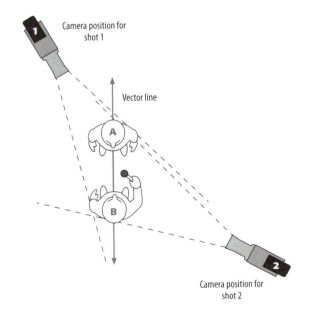
16

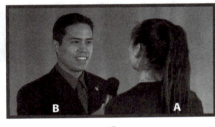
17

Also indicate whether continuity is (18) *good* or (19) *bad*.

a. camera setup A

Camera position for shot 1

Vector line

A

B

Camera position for shot 2

2a ◯ ◯ ◯ ◯
14 15 16 17

◯   ◯
18   19

P A G E
T O T A L

PHOTOS: EDWARD AIONA

© 2012 Wadsworth, Cengage Learning

c. cutting from camera 2 to a different point of view of the university president and her husband during a reception

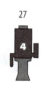

27

28

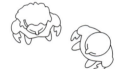

29

30

3c ◯ ◯ ◯ ◯
27 28 29 30

3d ◯   ◯   ◯
31   32   33

P A G E
T O T A L

d. cutting from two-shots of piano player and singer to CUs

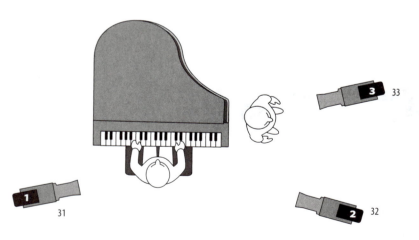

3

33

1

31

2

32

W-256

© 2012 Wadsworth, Cengage Learning

4. In the following diagram of a simple interview, select the two cameras that will facilitate optimal cross-shooting and fill in the bubbles with the corresponding numbers.

4 ◯ ◯ ◯ ◯
  34 35 36 37

34

Host

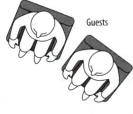

Guests

4

37

2

35

3

36

P A G E
T O T A L

© 2012 Wadsworth, Cengage Learning

5. From the nine frame grabs of source clips below, select four shots to tell the story of a woman getting into her car and driving off. Fill in the bubbles with the numbers of the shots you selected in the order you would edit them together.

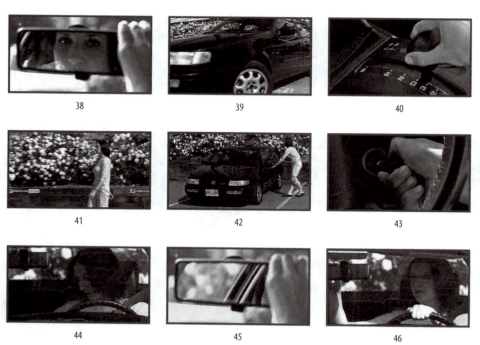

38

39

40

41

42

43

44

45

46

a. shot 1

b. shot 2

c. shot 3

d. shot 4

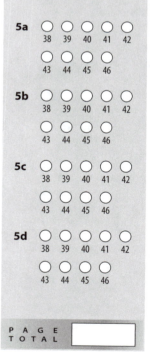

5a
 ○ ○ ○ ○ ○
 38 39 40 41 42
 ○ ○ ○ ○
 43 44 45 46

5b
 ○ ○ ○ ○ ○
 38 39 40 41 42
 ○ ○ ○ ○
 43 44 45 46

5c
 ○ ○ ○ ○ ○
 38 39 40 41 42
 ○ ○ ○ ○
 43 44 45 46

5d
 ○ ○ ○ ○ ○
 38 39 40 41 42
 ○ ○ ○ ○
 43 44 45 46

P A G E
T O T A L

PHOTOS: CENGAGE LEARNING

© 2012 Wadsworth, Cengage Learning

PHOTOS: EDWARD AIONA

PHOTOS: EDWARD AIONA

PHOTOS: JOHN VELTRI

PHOTOS: EDWARD AIONA

© 2012 Wadsworth, Cengage Learning

Course No. _____ Date _____ Name _____

6. For each of the following shot sequences, fill in the appropriate bubbles to indicate whether the sequence (47) *maintains* or (48) *disturbs* the mental map. If the mental map is disturbed, also indicate whether the major reason is a (49) *position switch* or a (50) *vector problem*. **(Multiple answers are possible.)**

a.
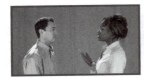 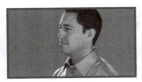 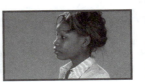

Shot 1 | Shot 2 | Shot 3

6a ○ 47 ○ 48
       ○ 49 ○ 50

b.
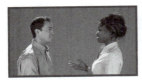 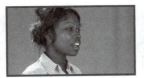 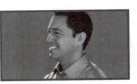

Shot 1 | Shot 2 | Shot 3

6b ○ 47 ○ 48
       ○ 49 ○ 50

c.
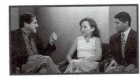 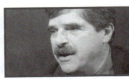 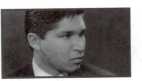

Shot 1 | Shot 2 | Shot 3

6c ○ 47 ○ 48
       ○ 49 ○ 50

d.
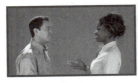 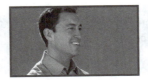 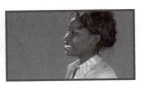

Shot 1 | Shot 2 | Shot 3

6d ○ 47 ○ 48
       ○ 49 ○ 50

PAGE TOTAL

SECTION TOTAL

CHAPTER 20   EDITING FUNCTIONS AND PRINCIPLES

REVIEW OF COMPLEXITY EDITING

Select the correct answers and fill in the bubbles with the corresponding numbers.

1. The simultaneity of several separate events can best be shown with (51) *multiple screens* (52) *flashbacks* (53) *flashforwards.*

2. In complexity editing, a jump cut (54) *clearly signals an editing mistake* (55) *should never be used* (56) *can be used as an intensifier.*

3. A series of quick cuts between camera 1 and camera 2 in the figure below would be appropriate in (57) *continuity editing only* (58) *both continuity and complexity editing* (59) *instantaneous editing.*

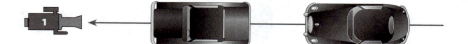

4. A filmic shorthand in which a rhythmic series of seemingly unrelated shots generates new meaning is called a (60) *montage* (61) *clip* (62) *sequence.*

5. Complexity editing (63) *can occasionally break with continuity principles* (64) *must adhere to continuity principles* (65) *does not consider continuity principles.*

6. In complexity editing, DVE (66) *should be avoided* (67) *can be used to intensify a scene* (68) *can be used to clarify a scene.*

1	○ 51	○ 52	○ 53
2	○ 54	○ 55	○ 56
3	○ 57	○ 58	○ 59
4	○ 60	○ 61	○ 62
5	○ 63	○ 64	○ 65
6	○ 66	○ 67	○ 68

PAGE TOTAL

© 2012 Wadsworth, Cengage Learning

7. Assuming that you intend to construct a montage of a car fleeing the police, quick cuts among all four cameras shown in the figure below would be appropriate (69) *in continuity editing* (70) *in complexity editing* (71) *under no circumstances.*

7   ○   ○   ○
    69   70   71

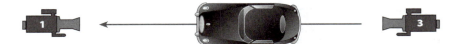

8. In the context of continuity editing, cutting from shot 1 to shot 2 as shown below is (72) *acceptable* (73) *unacceptable* because (74) *the motion vectors are continuing* (75) *the edit would cause a jump cut.*

8   ○   ○
    72   73
    ○   ○
    74   75

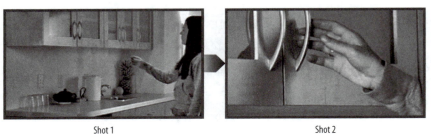

Shot 1   Shot 2

P A G E
T O T A L

SECTION
T O T A L

PHOTOS: CENGAGE LEARNING

© 2012 Wadsworth, Cengage Learning

Mark the following statements as true or false by filling in the bubbles in the **T** (for true) or **F** (for false) column.

		T	F
1.	The vector line extends from the camera to the horizon.	**1** ◯ 76	◯ 77
2.	When cutting from an MS to a CU of somebody sitting down, continuity is best preserved by cutting after the person is seated.	**2** ◯ 78	◯ 79
3.	A blurred still shot of a car represents a motion vector.	**3** ◯ 80	◯ 81
4.	Somebody pointing at an object constitutes an index vector.	**4** ◯ 82	◯ 83
5.	Editing must always be done in the context of ethics—the principles of right conduct.	**5** ◯ 84	◯ 85
6.	If the move is properly motivated, the vector line can be crossed in continuity editing.	**6** ◯ 86	◯ 87
7.	Two of the major editing functions are to shorten and to combine.	**7** ◯ 88	◯ 89
8.	Subject continuity means that we can recognize a person from one shot to the next.	**8** ◯ 90	◯ 91
9.	A cutaway can be any shot so long as it does not project a vector.	**9** ◯ 92	◯ 93
10.	Index and motion vectors play an important role in continuity editing.	**10** ◯ 94	◯ 95
11.	So long as we can recognize a person, it does not matter even in continuity editing that she appears on screen-left in one shot and on screen-right in the next.	**11** ◯ 96	◯ 97
12.	Ethical considerations are the purview of the director and have no place in the busy news editing room.	**12** ◯ 98	◯ 99
13.	A shrinking circle wipe is an especially effective way to close a documentary on a flood disaster.	**13** ◯ 100	◯ 101
14.	A jump cut occurs when the subject has moved his head even slightly from one shot to the next.	**14** ◯ 102	◯ 103
15.	A jump cut may be used effectively in complexity editing.	**15** ◯ 104	◯ 105
16.	Sound is an important factor in maintaining continuity.	**16** ◯ 106	◯ 107
17.	A mental map helps viewers to organize on- and off-screen space.	**17** ◯ 108	◯ 109

SECTION TOTAL [   ]

© 2012 Wadsworth, Cengage Learning

■ PROBLEM-SOLVING APPLICATIONS

1. Select a scene from any type of television show or film that demonstrates complexity editing. Be specific.

2. Use a camcorder and ad-lib a scene in which your crossing the line contributes to an intensified experience.

3. The news director encourages you to use a peel effect for transitions in a headline news teaser. What is your reaction? Be specific.

4. The staging for a presidential debate shows two candidates side by side, facing the audience; a moderator is in the middle, facing the candidates, with his back to the audience. The primary cameras are located in the audience, pointing at the stage. One camera is backstage, exactly opposite the moderator. It is to get three-shots in which we see the backs of the candidates and the moderator as he addresses the candidates. Assuming that the objective is seamless continuity, do you have any concerns about this setup? Be specific.

5. The producer tells you not to worry about using a stock shot of videographers for a necessary cutaway in the editing of a news conference. What is your reaction? Be specific.

© 2012 Wadsworth, Cengage Learning

© 2012 Wadsworth, Cengage Learning

Scale: ¼" = 1'

Property List

© 2012 Wadsworth, Cengage Learning

Scale: ¼" = 1'

Property List

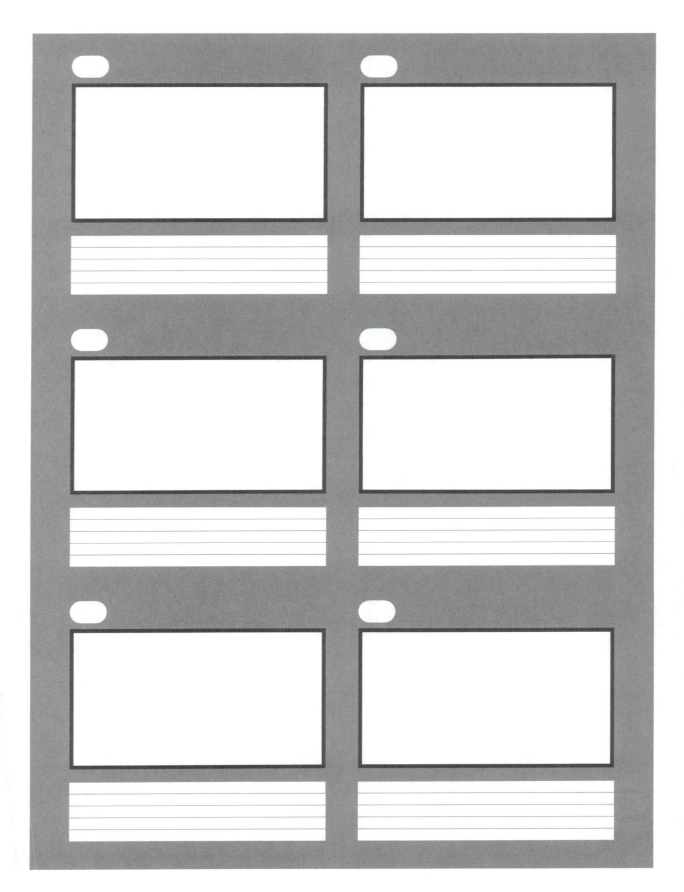

© 2012 Wadsworth, Cengage Learning

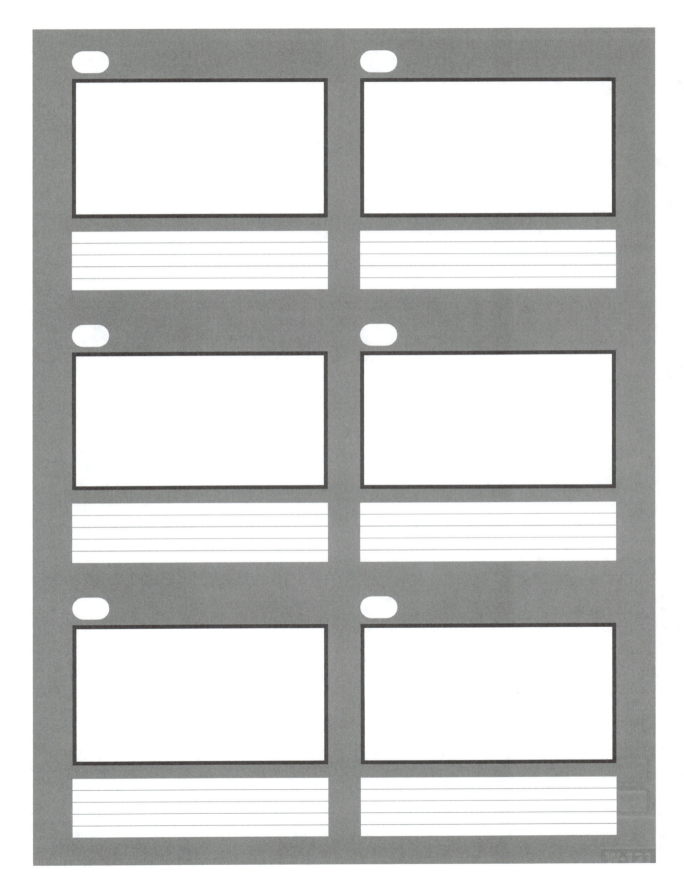

© 2012 Wadsworth, Cengage Learning